Rust for N

Programming and Automation

Second Edition

Work around designing networks, TCP/IP protocol, packet analysis and performance monitoring using Rust 1.68

Gilbert Stew

Published by: GitforGits

Publisher: Sonal Dhandre

www.gitforgits.com

support@gitforgits.com

Printed in India

First Printing: June 2024

ISBN: 9788119177349

Cover Design by: Kitten Publishing

For permission to use material from this book, please contact GitforGits at support@gitforgits.com.

Prologue

Welcome to the second edition of "Rust for Network Programming and Automation." Hi, I'm Gilbert Stew, and I'm very excited to show you how to use Rust 1.68 to navigate the ever-changing world of network programming. This edition fills in the gaps and expectations from the first edition, providing more depth, clarity, and updated content to help you master network programming and automation.

When I first started writing this book, I wanted to create a resource that demystified network programming and made it accessible to both new and experienced developers. Rust's robust capabilities make it an excellent platform for developing efficient, reliable, and secure network applications. This second edition builds on the foundation laid by the first, incorporating feedback from readers and my own evolving understanding of the lessons learned from it.

In this new edition, we begin with the fundamentals of TCP/IP, the protocol suite that underpins the internet. Understanding TCP/IP is critical, and I will ensure that you understand the fundamentals, from IP addressing and subnetting to packet transmission. We then look at how to create and manage network connections in Rust, using the standard library and popular crates like Tokio and Mio for asynchronous networking. Packet analysis is another essential component of network programming. I show you how to capture and analyze network traffic using libraries such as pnet and libtins. These tools enable you to inspect packets, understand their structure, and extract useful data for troubleshooting and security analysis. You will learn how to set up packet capture loops, process and analyze packets, and gain insights into network behavior.

One of the most significant updates in this edition is the thorough coverage of network automation, which recognizes that automation is critical for efficiently managing complex networks. I introduce you to Rust libraries and techniques for automating network tasks, such as IP configuration and AWS virtual private clouds (VPC) management, using the rusoto crate. You'll also learn how to set up VPNs, which improve your network's security and connectivity. Data center networking is another critical area we investigate. You will learn how to configure and manage data center networks, ensuring that they run smoothly and securely. The book also covers cloud network configuration, guiding you through the process of creating and managing virtual private clouds (VPCs), which is an essential skill in today's cloud-based world.

Monitoring and maintaining network performance is critical, and this edition covers the subject extensively. You will learn how to use Rust and libraries such as notify-rust to monitor network availability, latency, packet loss, and jitter. These abilities are critical for ensuring that your network runs smoothly and identifying problems before they escalate. Security is interwoven throughout the book, emphasizing the significance of developing secure network applications. From secure socket programming to detecting network threats via packet analysis and monitoring, I ensure you are prepared to face modern security challenges.

I worked hard to fill the gaps from the first edition, incorporating your feedback and refining the content to meet your expectations. This second edition promises a more comprehensive, engaging, and practical approach to learning network programming and automation with Rust.

Regards,

Gilbert Stew

Content

Preface

Designed with the needs of those interested in network programming and automation in mind, this updated "Rust for Network Programming and Automation" explores the realism of network programming within the robust Rust ecosystem. Building on top of Rust 1.68, this book takes you step-by-step through the essentials of network protocols, packet analysis, and network administration with up-to-date and thorough material.

Starting with the fundamentals of TCP/IP, you will be introduced to the core principles of network communication, such as data packet structure and transmission. The book then moves on to cover important topics like IP addressing, subnetting, and gateway configuration, ensuring a thorough understanding of network fundamentals. The chapters focus on the practical aspects of network programming, particularly the use of popular Rust libraries such as Tokio, Mio, and Rust-async for asynchronous network programming. These libraries are thoroughly examined, demonstrating how to create TCP listeners, bind sockets, and handle incoming connections efficiently.

Packet manipulation and analysis are also important topics, with practical examples using libraries like pnet and libtins. You will learn how to capture, process, and analyze network packets to gain an understanding of network traffic and identify potential problems. The book also focuses on network and performance monitoring, showing you how to set up and use various tools to track network availability, utilization, latency, packet loss, and jitter. Understanding these metrics allows you to ensure optimal network performance and reliability. Cloud network configuration, VPN setup, and data center networking are thoroughly covered, providing the necessary knowledge to manage and automate complex network environments.

Each chapter is intended to build on the previous one, resulting in a coherent and comprehensive learning experience. With clear explanations, practical examples, and up-to-date content, "Rust for Network Programming and Automation" provides you with the skills you need to get started in network programming and automation with the most recent Rust release. Anyone looking to learn Rust for network-centric applications can use this book, as it covers the basics as well as advanced topics.

In this book you will learn how to:

- Become fluent in the fundamentals of Rust-based TCP/IP programming.

- Use the pnet and libtins libraries to capture and analyze packets in depth.

- Use the Rust-async, Tokio, and Mio libraries to program asynchronous networks efficiently.

- Be well-versed in IP addressing, subnetting, and configuring gateways to assure a secure network installation.

- Learn to use Rust and OpenVPN to set up VPN connections.

- Get skilled in monitoring network availability, latency, and packet loss.

- Optimize network performance and uptime by automating routine tasks and configurations.

- Apply sophisticated Rust methods to the configuration and management of data center networks.

- Utilize AWS and rusoto to establish and oversee VPCs.

- Use packet analysis and monitoring to improve network security by identifying threats.

GitforGits

Prerequisites

This book offers a systematic, practical method to learn Rust for network applications, right form the basics to sufficient knowledge, making it ideal for anyone interested in network programming or new to the subject. In this book, I will show you to use Rust to its maximum capacity to learn the basics of programming networks.

Codes Usage

Are you in need of some helpful code examples to assist you in your programming and documentation? Look no further! Our book offers a wealth of supplemental material, including code examples and exercises.

Not only is this book here to aid you in getting your job done, but you have our permission to use the example code in your programs and documentation. However, please note that if you are reproducing a significant portion of the code, we do require you to contact us for permission.

But don't worry, using several chunks of code from this book in your program or answering a question by citing our book and quoting example code does not require permission. But if you do choose to give credit, an attribution typically includes the title, author, publisher, and ISBN. For example, "Rust for Network Programming and Automation, Second Edition by Gilbert Stew".

If you are unsure whether your intended use of the code examples falls under fair use or the permissions outlined above, please do not hesitate to reach out to us at support@gitforgits.com.

We are happy to assist and clarify any concerns.

Acknowledgement

I owe a tremendous debt of gratitude to GitforGits, for their unflagging enthusiasm and wise counsel throughout the entire process of writing this book. Their knowledge and careful editing helped make sure the piece was useful for people of all reading levels and comprehension skills. In addition, I'd like to thank everyone involved in the publishing process for their efforts in making this book a reality. Their efforts, from copyediting to advertising, made the project what it is today.

Finally, I'd like to express my gratitude to everyone who has shown me unconditional love and encouragement throughout my life. Their support was crucial to the completion of this book. I appreciate your help with this endeavour and your continued interest in my career.

CHAPTER 1: BASICS OF NETWORK AUTOMATION

Need of Network Automation

Network automation employs software tools and technologies to streamline and automate the management, configuration, and operation of computer networks. By leveraging machine learning, artificial intelligence, and orchestration, network automation enhances efficiency, accuracy, and security in network operations.

Evolution of Network Management

Network automation has significantly evolved over the years. Initially, network management relied heavily on manual intervention through basic scripting and command-line interfaces, a process both time-consuming and prone to errors. As networks expanded, managing them using traditional methods became increasingly challenging.

Manual Processes

In the early days, network engineers used manual processes for network management. Basic scripts and command-line tools like ifconfig and netstat were common. These methods required extensive manual intervention, making the process laborious and error-prone. Network changes, configurations, and troubleshooting were all done manually, which was feasible for smaller, simpler networks but became untenable as network size and complexity grew.

Introduction of Network Management Systems (NMS)

The 1990s saw the advent of network management systems (NMS). These systems marked the beginning of network automation, providing centralized management and monitoring of networks. Tools like HP OpenView and IBM Tivoli allowed network engineers to monitor network performance, manage configurations, and detect issues from a single interface. NMS reduced manual intervention, improved efficiency, and provided valuable insights into network operations through data collection and analysis.

Rise of SDN and NFV

The 2000s introduced software-defined networking (SDN) and network functions virtualization (NFV), revolutionizing network automation. SDN separated the control plane from the data plane, allowing for centralized network control and easier management. NFV virtualized network services, enabling them to run on commodity hardware rather than specialized devices. These technologies abstracted network resources from physical hardware, offering greater flexibility and reducing the need for manual configuration.

SDN and NFV paved the way for more sophisticated automation. For instance, network configurations and policies could be applied dynamically across the network, responding to real-time demands without manual input. These advancements significantly reduced operational costs and increased network agility.

Beginning of Cloud Computing

With the advent of cloud computing, the need for network automation became even more pronounced. Cloud environments are highly dynamic, with resources such as virtual machines and containers constantly being provisioned, scaled, and decommissioned. Manual network management in such environments is impractical.

Automation tools in the cloud use machine learning and artificial intelligence to detect and respond to changes automatically. Tools like Ansible, Puppet, and Chef enable automated provisioning, configuration management, and orchestration, ensuring that network resources are optimally configured and managed. Machine learning algorithms analyze network traffic patterns, predict potential issues, and recommend or implement corrective actions, enhancing network reliability and performance.

Necessity and Rise of Network Automation

Several factors drive the demand for network automation in businesses, including increased network complexity, the need for greater agility, cost and time savings, cybersecurity, employee productivity, business continuity, and cloud adoption.

Network Complexity

Modern networks are more complex than ever, incorporating various devices, applications, and services that require intricate configuration and management. According to a survey by Enterprise Management Associates, 82% of organizations reported increased network complexity over the past five years. This complexity necessitates automation to manage networks effectively and reduce the risk of configuration errors.

Time and Cost Savings

Network automation offers significant time and cost savings. Juniper Networks reported that automation could reduce the time required for routine network configuration tasks by up to 90%. Automation minimizes manual interventions, reducing labor costs and the potential for human error, which can lead to costly network downtime.

Greater Agility

In today's fast-paced business environment, agility is crucial. Businesses must quickly adapt to market changes, and network automation facilitates this adaptability. A study by Enterprise Management Associates found that businesses using network automation could respond to network infrastructure changes up to ten times faster than those that did not.

Cybersecurity

With the rising threat of cybersecurity attacks, network automation becomes essential in enhancing security postures. The Ponemon Institute reported that 75% of businesses believe automation improves cybersecurity. Automated tools can quickly detect and respond to security threats, apply security patches, and ensure compliance with security policies, significantly reducing the risk of breaches.

Employee Productivity

Automation frees IT staff from repetitive, routine tasks, allowing them to focus on more strategic activities. According to a survey by Network World, 75% of IT professionals believe that network automation improves employee productivity. By automating mundane tasks, employees can devote more time to innovation and optimization.

Business Continuity

Downtime is costly for businesses, and network automation helps ensure continuous operations. Cisco reported that businesses using network automation experienced 60% less downtime compared to those that did not. Automated systems can quickly detect and resolve issues, maintain network health, and ensure uninterrupted service delivery.

Cloud Adoption

As cloud adoption rises, network automation becomes critical in managing cloud infrastructures efficiently. The Cloud Security Alliance found that 50% of businesses use network automation to manage their cloud networks. Automated tools help in provisioning, scaling, and managing cloud resources, ensuring optimal performance and security.

Opportunities for Today and Future

The growing prominence of network automation has created numerous career opportunities. Key roles include:

Network Automation Engineer

Responsible for developing and implementing automation tools and scripts to manage network processes. They design automated solutions, analyze network performance, and troubleshoot automation-related issues. Proficiency in network protocols, scripting languages, and tools like Ansible and Python is essential.

Network Automation Architect

Designs and implements the overall network automation strategy for an organization. They develop policies, procedures, and standards, ensuring alignment with business objectives. Deep knowledge of network architecture, automation tools, and best practices is crucial.

Network Automation Developer

Focuses on developing software applications and tools to automate network management processes. They write code to automate tasks, develop software modules, and integrate third-party tools. Expertise in software development and automation tools like Ansible and Python is required.

Network Automation Analyst

Analyzes network performance data to identify automation opportunities. They monitor network activity, pinpoint areas for improvement, and recommend automation solutions. Skills in network analytics, data analysis, and automation tools are necessary.

Network Automation Manager

Oversees the development and implementation of network automation solutions. They manage teams of engineers and developers, develop policies and standards, and ensure solutions align with business goals. Expertise in network architecture, automation tools, and project management is needed.

Cloud Automation Engineer

Develops and implements automation solutions for cloud infrastructure management. They design automated solutions for cloud platforms like AWS, Azure, and Google Cloud, analyze performance data, and troubleshoot automation issues. Understanding of cloud architecture, scripting languages, and tools like Terraform and Ansible is essential.

As network technologies advance, the demand for qualified individuals in network automation will only increase, creating interesting opportunities for those who are passionate about technology and automation.

Types of Network Automation

Network automation is the process of automating the configuration, management, and monitoring of network devices and services. There are several types of network automation, each with their own specific applications and benefits. Following are the four types of network automation and provides examples of each type of automation function.

Configuration Automation

Configuration automation is the process of automating the configuration of network devices such as switches, routers, and firewalls. This type of automation can save time and reduce errors that can occur during manual configuration. Configuration automation can be broken down into two subtypes: configuration management and configuration drift detection.

Configuration Management

Configuration management refers to the process of defining and managing configurations across multiple network devices. Configuration management tools such as Ansible, Puppet, and Chef can be used to automate the configuration of network devices in a data center. These tools provide a way to define configuration templates for specific devices and apply those configurations across multiple devices simultaneously. For example, an Ansible playbook can be defined to configure multiple routers with specific IP addresses, access control lists, and routing protocols.

Configuration Drift Detection

Configuration drift detection refers to the process of detecting and remedying any configuration changes that deviate from the baseline configuration. Configuration drift detection tools such as Rudder and NCM can be used to detect any unauthorized changes that may impact the security or performance of the network. These tools can also be used to automatically remediate any drift detected in the network configuration.

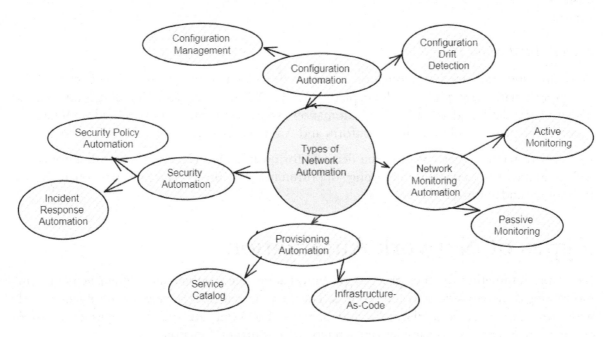

Fig 1.1 Applications of Network Automation

Network Monitoring Automation

Network monitoring automation is the process of automating the collection and analysis of network performance data. This type of automation can help network administrators identify issues and optimize network performance. Network monitoring automation can be broken down into two subtypes: active monitoring and passive monitoring.

Active Monitoring

Active monitoring refers to the process of proactively sending test packets across the network to identify and troubleshoot network performance issues. Active monitoring tools such as Pingdom and Nagios can be used to monitor network devices and their connectivity to other devices. These tools can also be used to monitor the availability of network services such as HTTP, FTP, and DNS.

Passive Monitoring

Passive monitoring refers to the process of monitoring network traffic in real-time to identify and troubleshoot network performance issues. Passive monitoring tools such as Wireshark and Tcpdump can be used to capture and analyze network traffic. These tools can help network administrators identify the root cause of network performance issues and take the necessary steps to resolve them.

Provisioning Automation

Provisioning automation is the process of automating the provisioning of new network devices and services. This type of automation can help reduce the time it takes to deploy new services and can reduce the likelihood of errors during the provisioning process. Provisioning automation can be broken down into two subtypes: infrastructure-as-code and service catalog.

Infrastructure-As-Code

Infrastructure-as-code refers to the process of defining network infrastructure through code that can be versioned and tested, just like software. Infrastructure-as-code tools such as Terraform and CloudFormation can be used to provision new virtual machines in a cloud environment. These tools allow network administrators to define an infrastructure-as-code template that specifies the resources required to deploy a new virtual machine, and then automatically provision those resources and configure the virtual machine with the desired software and settings.

Service Catalog

Service catalog refers to the process of defining and publishing standardized service offerings for network services. Service catalog tools such as OpenStack and Azure Resource Manager can be used to define and publish service offerings for network services. These tools allow network administrators to define a service catalog that includes preconfigured network services such as load balancing, virtual private networks, and firewalls. End users can then select the desired service from the service catalog, and the system will automatically provision the required resources and configure the service.

Security Automation

Security automation is the process of automating the detection, analysis, and response to security threats. This type of automation can help reduce the time it takes to identify and respond to security incidents, thereby reducing the risk of data breaches and network downtime. Security automation can be broken down into two subtypes: security policy automation and incident response automation.

Security Policy Automation

Security policy automation refers to the process of automating the creation, enforcement, and validation of security policies across the network. Security policy automation tools such as Tufin and AlgoSec can be used to automate the process of defining and enforcing security policies across the network. These tools allow network administrators to define security policies in a central location and then automatically push those policies out to all network devices.

Incident Response Automation

Incident response automation refers to the process of automating the detection and response to security incidents. Incident response automation tools such as Demisto and Phantom can be used to automate the process of identifying security incidents, analyzing them to determine the appropriate response, and then executing that response automatically. For example, if a security incident is detected, the tool can automatically isolate the affected device from the network, block the malicious traffic, and then notify the security team.

Software Defined Networks

Understanding SDN Architecture

Software Defined Networking (SDN) is an approach to network architecture that allows network administrators to manage and optimize network traffic flows using software applications rather than relying on traditional network devices such as switches and routers. SDN enables the centralization and programmability of network management, which allows for greater flexibility, efficiency, and agility in network operations.

At the core of SDN is the separation of the network control plane from the data plane. In traditional networking, the control plane is embedded in each network device, such as a switch or router, and is responsible for making routing and forwarding decisions. The data plane, on the other hand, is responsible for actually forwarding data packets through the network. In an SDN architecture, the control plane is separated from the data plane and is centralized in a software controller that communicates with the network devices using a standard protocol called OpenFlow. The data plane remains in the network devices and forwards data packets according to the decisions made by the controller.

The benefits of SDN are numerous. First, SDN enables the automation and orchestration of network functions, which allows for faster provisioning of network services, easier scalability, and more agile response to changing network demands. Second, SDN enables network administrators to create and enforce network policies in a centralized manner, which makes it easier to manage and control network traffic flows. Third, SDN can improve network performance by enabling traffic engineering, load balancing, and traffic shaping. Finally, SDN can reduce network operational costs by simplifying network management and allowing for more efficient use of network resources.

There are several components to an SDN architecture. The first component is the software controller, which is responsible for managing and programming the network devices. The controller communicates with the network devices using the OpenFlow protocol and makes forwarding decisions based on network policies and traffic conditions. The second component is the OpenFlow switch, which is a network device that is capable of being programmed by the controller. OpenFlow switches provide the data plane functionality in an SDN architecture. The third component is the SDN applications, which are software applications that run on top of the controller and can perform various network functions such as traffic engineering, load balancing, and security.

Types of SDN

There are three main types of Software Defined Networking (SDN), each with its unique features and use cases.

Centralized SDN

Centralized SDN is the most common type of SDN, where a single software controller manages the entire network. This architecture is best suited for large, complex networks where managing and coordinating network traffic flows across multiple devices can be challenging. Centralized SDN allows for a more efficient and agile network infrastructure since it provides a single point of control for the network. An example of a centralized SDN architecture is the Open Network Operating System (ONOS) project.

Distributed SDN

In distributed SDN, multiple controllers are used to manage different parts of the network. This architecture is particularly useful in networks that are geographically dispersed or have multiple tenants with different network policies. Distributed SDN enables more effective resource utilization and can also improve network reliability by providing redundancy. An example of a distributed SDN architecture is the Floodlight OpenFlow Controller.

Hybrid SDN

Hybrid SDN combines both centralized and distributed SDN architectures. This architecture is particularly useful in networks that have both centralized and distributed components, such as cloud-based networks. Hybrid SDN allows network administrators to take advantage of the benefits of both architectures and to create a network infrastructure that is tailored to their specific needs. An example of a hybrid SDN architecture is the OpenDaylight project.

In addition to the three main types of SDN, there are also several SDN technologies and platforms that provide various SDN functionalities. Some examples of these technologies and platforms include:

OpenFlow

OpenFlow is a protocol that allows for the centralized control of network traffic flows. It is used in many SDN architectures to provide a standard communication protocol between the controller and network devices.

Virtualization

Virtualization is a technology that allows network administrators to create virtual networks that run on top of a physical network. This enables greater network agility and allows for more efficient use of network resources.

Network Functions Virtualization (NFV)

NFV is a technology that allows network functions, such as firewalls and load balancers, to be virtualized and run on commodity hardware. This allows network administrators to create a more flexible and scalable network infrastructure.

To conclude, the different types of SDN provide network administrators with a range of options for designing and managing their network infrastructure. Whether it is a centralized, distributed, or hybrid SDN architecture, each has its unique features and use cases. Additionally, the different SDN technologies and platforms provide further options for achieving network agility, efficiency, and flexibility.

Network Protocols

Network protocols are the rules and procedures that govern the communication between devices on a computer network. In essence, network protocols define the way in which devices communicate with each other over a network, including how data is transmitted, received, and interpreted. They are an essential part of modern network infrastructure, allowing devices to communicate with each other in a standardized, reliable, and secure way.

The Role of Network Protocols

Network protocols play a fundamental role in enabling communication within and between networks. These protocols define rules and conventions for data exchange, ensuring smooth and efficient communication between devices. Let us explore the critical roles and importance of network protocols in modern networking.

Standardization

Network protocols provide a standardized way for devices to communicate, ensuring compatibility and interoperability across different manufacturers and operating systems. This standardization is crucial because it allows diverse hardware and software components to function together seamlessly. For example, regardless of whether a device is running on Windows, Linux, or macOS, protocols like TCP/IP ensure that data transmission remains consistent and reliable. Standardization also simplifies network design and management, as network administrators can rely on well-defined protocols to maintain and troubleshoot networks.

Reliability

Protocols play a vital role in ensuring the reliability of network communications. They include mechanisms for error detection and correction, which help to minimize data loss and errors during transmission. For instance, the Transmission Control Protocol (TCP) provides reliability by establishing a connection between devices before data transfer and ensuring that all packets are received in the correct order. If any packet is lost or corrupted during transmission, TCP will retransmit the packet, ensuring that the recipient receives the complete and accurate data.

Security

Security is another critical aspect of network protocols. They provide mechanisms for encryption, authentication, and access control, which are essential for protecting data and maintaining network integrity. Protocols like Secure Sockets Layer (SSL) and Transport Layer Security (TLS) encrypt data during transmission, preventing unauthorized access and tampering. Authentication protocols, such as Kerberos, ensure that only authorized users can access network resources. By implementing these security measures, network protocols help safeguard sensitive information and prevent cyber threats.

Importance of Network Protocols

Network protocols are indispensable to the functioning of modern network infrastructure. They ensure seamless communication, scalability, and flexibility, making them fundamental to network operations.

Interoperability

Interoperability is a key benefit of network protocols. They enable devices from different manufacturers and operating systems to communicate with each other, fostering a diverse and interconnected network environment. This interoperability is essential for integrating various devices, from computers and smartphones to IoT devices, within a unified network. For instance, the Internet Protocol (IP) allows devices worldwide to communicate, regardless of their underlying technology.

Scalability

Network protocols support scalability, allowing networks to grow and accommodate more devices, data, and higher traffic volumes. Protocols like IP and Ethernet are designed to handle network expansion, ensuring that adding new devices or increasing data flow does not compromise network performance. Scalability is crucial for businesses and service providers that need to scale their networks to meet growing demand without overhauling existing infrastructure.

Flexibility

Flexibility is another important characteristic of network protocols. They allow network administrators to choose and implement protocols that best suit their specific network environments and requirements. For example, administrators can use TCP for applications requiring high reliability and UDP for time-sensitive applications like video streaming, where speed is more critical than error correction. This flexibility enables the optimization of network performance and resource utilization based on specific needs.

Types of Network Protocols

There are numerous network protocols, each serving distinct functions and applications. Following are some of the most widely used protocols:

Transmission Control Protocol/Internet Protocol (TCP/IP)

TCP/IP is the foundational protocol suite for the Internet and most other networks. It defines how data is transmitted, routed, and received across networks. TCP ensures reliable data transfer with error checking and correction, while IP handles addressing and routing of packets to their destination. Together, TCP/IP provides a robust framework for network communication, supporting a wide range of applications and services.

User Datagram Protocol (UDP)

UDP is a simpler, faster protocol than TCP, often used for time-sensitive applications such as video and audio streaming. Unlike TCP, UDP does not establish a connection before data transfer and lacks error checking and correction mechanisms, making it less reliable but faster. This trade-off is beneficial for applications where speed is critical, and occasional data loss is acceptable.

File Transfer Protocol (FTP)

FTP is used for transferring files between computers on a network. It allows users to upload and download files from remote servers and includes mechanisms for authentication and access control. FTP is widely used for file sharing and data exchange, though it has largely been replaced by more secure protocols like SFTP (Secure File Transfer Protocol) and FTPS (FTP Secure).

Simple Mail Transfer Protocol (SMTP)

SMTP is used for sending email over the Internet. It defines how email messages are transmitted and received, including mechanisms for authentication and encryption. SMTP servers relay email messages from the sender to the recipient's email server, ensuring reliable and efficient email delivery.

Hypertext Transfer Protocol (HTTP)

HTTP is the protocol used for accessing and retrieving data from web servers. It defines how data is formatted and transmitted over the Internet, enabling web browsers to display web pages. HTTPS, the secure version of HTTP, adds encryption to protect data during transmission, ensuring secure communication between clients and servers.

Specialized Network Protocols

In addition to the general-purpose protocols mentioned above, there are many specialized protocols designed for specific network functions:

Domain Name System (DNS)

DNS maps domain names to IP addresses, allowing users to access websites using human-readable addresses instead of numeric IP addresses. It functions like a phonebook for the Internet, translating domain names into the corresponding IP addresses required for data routing.

Border Gateway Protocol (BGP)

BGP is used for routing data between autonomous systems on the Internet. It determines the best paths for data to travel across the complex web of interconnected networks that make up the Internet. BGP plays a crucial role in maintaining the stability and efficiency of Internet routing.

Secure Shell (SSH)

SSH is a protocol for securely accessing and managing remote servers. It provides encrypted communication, ensuring that data transmitted between the client and server is protected from eavesdropping and tampering. SSH is widely used for remote administration and secure file transfers.

Network protocols facilitate interoperability across systems, let networks to scale as they grow, and give the flexibility required to react to changing network requirements. The significance and utility of network protocols will continue to increase in the future as both technology and networks evolve and diversify.

Network automation tools streamline various network management tasks, enhancing efficiency, reliability, and security. These tools fall into several categories, each serving a specific function in network automation.

Network Automation Tools & Categories

Configuration Management Tools

Configuration management tools automate the process of configuring network devices, ensuring consistency across the network. These tools simplify the deployment and management of network configurations, reducing the risk of human error and enhancing network reliability. By maintaining a centralized configuration repository, these tools enable network administrators to manage device settings and roll out changes efficiently across multiple devices.

Examples:

- Ansible: Uses simple, human-readable YAML templates to manage configurations and automate deployment processes.
- Puppet: Automates the delivery and operation of software across the entire infrastructure, ensuring consistency and compliance.
- Chef: Manages configurations using recipes written in Ruby, allowing for flexible and powerful automation.
- SaltStack: Provides event-driven IT automation and configuration management, supporting large-scale environments.

Network Monitoring Tools

Network monitoring tools provide real-time visibility into network health and performance. They continuously monitor network devices, traffic, and services, alerting administrators to potential issues. These tools help in identifying bottlenecks, outages, and performance degradations, enabling quick resolution before they impact users.

Examples:

- SolarWinds: Offers comprehensive network monitoring with detailed performance metrics and alerts.
- PRTG Network Monitor: Provides versatile and customizable network monitoring, supporting various sensors and devices.
- Nagios: An open-source solution that monitors network services, host resources, and infrastructure components.

Network Security Tools

Network security tools automate tasks related to network security, such as vulnerability scanning, penetration testing, and threat detection. These tools help in identifying and mitigating security risks by continuously scanning the network for vulnerabilities and suspicious activities, ensuring that security policies are enforced and updated.

Examples:

- Nessus: Conducts comprehensive vulnerability assessments, identifying potential security weaknesses in the network.

- Qualys: Offers cloud-based security and compliance solutions, automating vulnerability management and policy compliance.

- Metasploit: Provides a powerful framework for penetration testing, enabling security professionals to find and exploit vulnerabilities.

Network Performance Monitoring Tools

These tools focus on monitoring and analyzing network performance metrics to ensure optimal operation. They track parameters such as bandwidth usage, latency, packet loss, and throughput, helping administrators to proactively address performance issues and maintain high-quality service for end-users.

Examples:

- Dynatrace: Uses AI-driven analytics to provide deep insights into application and network performance.

- AppDynamics: Monitors application performance and user experience, linking network performance to business outcomes.

- Riverbed: Offers solutions for end-to-end network performance management, optimizing both physical and virtual networks.

Network Analytics Tools

Network analytics tools leverage advanced analytics techniques, including machine learning, to provide deep insights into network performance and usage patterns. These tools analyze vast amounts of network data to identify trends, anomalies, and potential issues, helping administrators to make data-driven decisions and optimize network operations.

Examples:

- Cisco DNA Analytics: Provides comprehensive network insights using machine learning to enhance performance and security.

- ExtraHop: Delivers real-time analytics for network and security operations, using machine learning to detect threats and performance issues.

- Nyansa: Utilizes advanced analytics to monitor network health, user experience, and device performance across complex environments.

Modern network infrastructure would not be complete without network automation tools, which allow administrators to streamline mundane processes, increase network reliability and efficiency, and tighten security measures. As networks get more complex, automation tools will play an increasingly important role in helping administrators scale and manage their networks more efficiently and with less human error.

Network Automation Architectures

When you set up, control, and keep an eye on your network infrastructure automatically, you are using network automation architecture. It's meant to make network operations easier, cut down on manual work, and boost speed and reliability. The architecture is made up of different parts that work together to make a full system for automating networks.

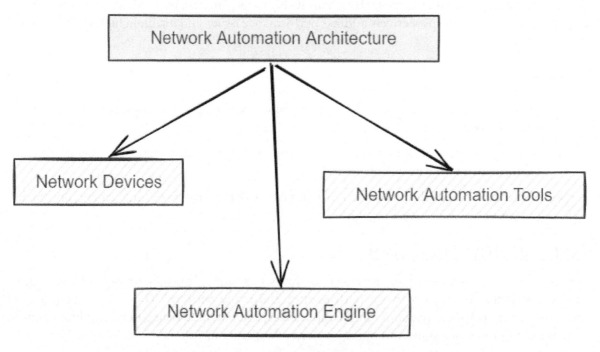

Fig 1.2: Network Automation Architecture

The key components of network automation architecture are:

Network Devices

Network devices are the building blocks of any network automation architecture. These devices

16

include routers, switches, firewalls, load balancers, and other network devices. They are responsible for managing the flow of data between network nodes and providing connectivity to the network. Network automation tools are used to automate the configuration and management of these devices.

There are a variety of network automation tools available for managing network devices. For example, tools like Ansible, Chef, and Puppet can be used to automate the configuration of network devices. These tools can be used to automate tasks such as configuring network interfaces, setting up VLANs, configuring routing protocols, and setting up security policies.

Network Automation Tools

Network automation tools are software applications designed to streamline and automate various network management tasks, such as configuration management, network monitoring, and network security. These tools interface with network devices to simplify management, improve performance, and mitigate errors and security vulnerabilities.

Configuration Management Tools

Configuration management tools automate the configuration and management of network devices. These tools enable network administrators to maintain consistent configurations across all devices, reducing the time and effort required for manual changes. Centralized management allows for quick deployment of configuration changes, minimizing downtime and ensuring compliance with organizational policies. Tools like Ansible, Puppet, Chef, and SaltStack are prominent examples, each offering unique features to cater to different network environments.

- Ansible: Uses YAML-based playbooks to automate configuration tasks, making it easy to manage and deploy configurations across a network.

- Puppet: Automates the delivery and operation of software, ensuring that all devices are configured correctly and consistently.

- Chef: Uses recipes written in Ruby to manage configurations, providing a powerful and flexible automation framework.

- SaltStack: Offers event-driven automation, allowing for real-time configuration management and orchestration.

Network Monitoring Tools

Network monitoring tools provide real-time insights into network traffic and performance. They continuously track various metrics, such as bandwidth usage, latency, and packet loss, and alert network administrators to potential issues before they escalate. This proactive monitoring helps maintain optimal network performance and reliability. Popular tools in this category include SolarWinds, PRTG Network Monitor, and Nagios.

- SolarWinds: Offers comprehensive monitoring capabilities, including detailed performance metrics and customizable alerts.

- PRTG Network Monitor: Supports a wide range of sensors and devices, providing versatile and scalable monitoring solutions.

- Nagios: An open-source tool that monitors network services, host resources, and infrastructure components, offering extensive customization options.

Security Management Tools

Security management tools focus on automating network security tasks, such as vulnerability scanning, threat detection, and access control. These tools help identify and mitigate security risks, ensuring that the network remains secure and compliant with security policies. Tools like Nessus, Qualys, and Metasploit are widely used for their robust security features.

- Nessus: Conducts comprehensive vulnerability assessments, identifying potential security weaknesses in the network.

- Qualys: Provides cloud-based security and compliance solutions, automating vulnerability management and policy compliance.

- Metasploit: Offers a powerful framework for penetration testing, enabling security professionals to find and exploit vulnerabilities.

Provisioning Tools

Provisioning tools automate the allocation of network resources to users and applications based on predefined policies and user roles. These tools streamline the process of resource management, ensuring that network resources are efficiently distributed and utilized. By automating provisioning, administrators can quickly respond to changing network demands and improve overall network efficiency.

- OpenStack: Manages large pools of compute, storage, and networking resources, allowing for flexible and scalable provisioning.

- VMware vSphere: Provides comprehensive virtualization and provisioning capabilities, enabling efficient resource management in virtualized environments.

- Cisco ACI: Automates network provisioning and management, integrating with various applications and services to enhance network agility.

Network automation tools offer numerous benefits, including improved efficiency, reduced operational costs, and enhanced security. Additionally, automation reduces the risk of human error, ensuring consistent and accurate network configurations and security policies. Real-time monitoring and proactive alerts help maintain network performance and reliability, while automated security measures protect against evolving threats.

Network Automation Engine

The network automation engine is the core of the network automation architecture. It includes a set of APIs and scripts that are used to automate network tasks. The engine can be used to automate tasks such as device discovery, configuration management, network monitoring, and network security.

The network automation engine can be used to automate a wide range of network tasks. For example, it can be used to automate the discovery of new network devices, automate the configuration of network devices, monitor network traffic and performance, and detect and prevent security threats.

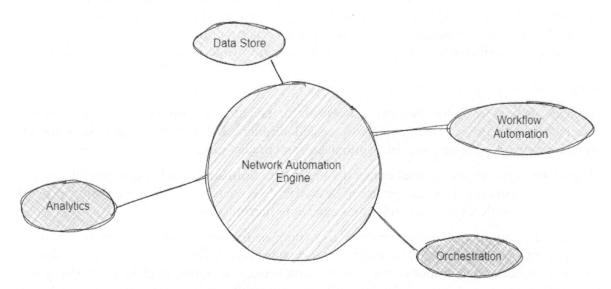

Fig 1.3 Network Automation Engine

Data Store

The data store is a centralized repository of network configuration data, network performance data, and network security data. The data store is used by the network automation engine to store and retrieve data that is used to automate network tasks.

The data store can be used to store a wide range of data related to network configuration, performance, and security. For example, it can store information about network devices, network topologies, network traffic, and security policies.

Workflow Automation

Workflow automation is used to automate network tasks by defining a set of rules and processes that are used to manage network devices. The workflow automation system is designed to automate tasks such as device discovery, device configuration, and network monitoring.

Workflow automation can be used to automate a wide range of network tasks. For example, it can be used to automate the discovery of new network devices, automate the configuration of network devices, monitor network traffic and performance, and detect and prevent security threats.

Orchestration

Orchestration is used to manage the overall network automation process. It is responsible for coordinating the activities of the network automation engine, data store, and workflow automation system. The orchestration system is used to ensure that network tasks are executed in the correct order and that they are completed within the specified timeframe.

Orchestration is critical to ensuring that network automation tasks are executed correctly and in a timely manner. It is responsible for coordinating the activities of different components of the network automation architecture. For example, the orchestration system can be used to ensure that network configuration changes are made in the correct order to avoid conflicts or errors.

Analytics

Analytics is used to analyze network performance data and to identify trends and patterns that can be used to improve network performance and reliability. The analytics system can be used to monitor network performance, detect anomalies, and predict future network behavior.

The analytics system can be used to identify network performance issues and to provide insights into network behavior. For example, it can be used to detect network congestion, identify network performance bottlenecks, and predict future network performance.

The architecture of network automation is a complex framework that encompasses multiple components collaborating to automate network functions. Every component has a distinct function in automating various elements of network management, including device configuration, network monitoring, and network security. Through the utilization of network automation tools and design, companies can effectively diminish the amount of time and exertion needed to oversee their networks, enhance network performance, and fortify network security.

Summary

In this chapter, we learned various components of network automation, including network automation tools, architectures, and types. We started by defining network automation, which is the use of software and tools to automate network management tasks. We discussed the benefits of network automation, including increased efficiency, reduced downtime, and improved security.

We then discussed the different types of network automation, including network configuration automation, network security automation, network monitoring automation, and network provisioning automation. For each type, we provided examples of automation tools and discussed their benefits. Next, we delved into network automation architecture, which involves several components working together to automate network tasks. We learned the different components of network automation architecture, including device management, orchestration, automation controllers, APIs, databases, and analytics. We also learned the role of each component and how they work together to automate network tasks.

We also learned software-defined networking (SDN), which is a type of network automation that uses software to manage and control network traffic. We provided an overview of SDN and learned the benefits of using SDN, such as increased flexibility, improved network management, and reduced costs. Furthermore, we explored network protocols and their role in network automation. We defined network protocols as a set of rules and standards that govern the communication between devices on a network. We also learned the different types of network protocols, such as TCP/IP, HTTP, and DNS, and their role in network automation.

Finally, we discussed the role of network automation tools in network automation architecture. We explained how network automation tools can be used to automate network tasks, including device configuration, network monitoring, and network security. We also discussed the benefits of using network automation tools, such as increased efficiency, reduced downtime, and improved security.

CHAPTER 2: ESSENTIALS OF LINUX FOR NETWORKS

Introduction to Networking Commands

Background

The network-related commands in Linux serve a crucial role in managing and configuring network interfaces, routing tables, network protocols, and services. These commands enable system administrators and developers to manage network-related tasks, such as setting up and managing network connections, troubleshooting network issues, and configuring network services.

Network interfaces are essential components of the networking system in Linux. They allow the system to connect to a network, and the network-related commands in Linux can be used to manage them. The ifconfig command is one of the most commonly used commands for managing network interfaces. It allows the administrator to view and configure network interfaces, including IP addresses, netmasks, and other network-related settings.

Routing tables are another critical component of the Linux networking system. They are used to determine the path that network packets should take to reach their destination. The route command is used to view and manage routing tables. It allows the administrator to add or remove routes, view the current routing table, and set default gateway addresses.

The Linux networking system supports various network protocols, including TCP/IP, UDP, ICMP, and others. The network-related commands in Linux allow administrators to manage these protocols, configure them, and troubleshoot issues related to them. For example, the netstat command can be used to view network statistics and information related to network protocols.

Network services, such as DNS, DHCP, and NTP, are crucial components of the Linux networking system. The network-related commands in Linux can be used to manage these services, including configuring and troubleshooting them. For example, the nslookup command is used to query DNS servers and resolve domain names to IP addresses.

In addition to the above, there are several other network-related commands in Linux that serve various purposes, such as monitoring network traffic, testing network connectivity, and configuring firewall rules.

Given below are some of the most commonly used network-related commands in Linux and their purposes:

- ping: This command is used to test network connectivity by sending ICMP echo requests to a remote host and waiting for a response.

- traceroute: This command is used to trace the path that network packets take from the source to the destination host, displaying each hop along the way.

- tcpdump: This command is used to capture and analyze network traffic, allowing administrators to troubleshoot network issues.

- iptables: This command is used to configure firewall rules to allow or block network traffic based on various criteria, such as source IP address, destination IP address, and protocol.

- ss: This command is used to view socket statistics, including open sockets, listening ports, and established connections.

Advantages of Network Commands

Network-related commands in Linux offer numerous benefits for system administrators and developers managing and configuring networked systems. These commands enhance efficiency, flexibility, security, and interoperability, making them indispensable tools in modern networking.

Efficient Network Management

Linux network commands streamline the management of network interfaces, routing tables, and protocols. They enable administrators to quickly view and configure network settings, saving time and minimizing the risk of errors. Commands like ifconfig and ip allow for rapid adjustments to network interfaces, while route and ip route facilitate efficient management of routing tables. This efficiency helps maintain a well-functioning network with minimal downtime.

Troubleshooting Network Issues

Powerful troubleshooting capabilities are a hallmark of Linux network commands. Tools like ping and traceroute provide essential diagnostics for network connectivity and path tracing. The ping command tests the reachability of a host on an IP network, helping to identify connectivity issues. The traceroute command reveals the route packets take to their destination, highlighting any points of failure or delay. These tools enable administrators to swiftly diagnose and resolve network problems, ensuring smooth network operations.

Flexibility and Customization

Linux network commands offer a high degree of flexibility and customization, allowing administrators to tailor network settings and services to specific needs. For example, iptables enables the configuration of firewall rules to control traffic based on criteria such as source and destination IP addresses and protocols. This flexibility extends to managing VPNs and other security measures, making it possible to create highly customized and secure network environments.

Secure Networking

Security is a critical concern in network management, and Linux commands provide robust tools to enhance network security. Commands like iptables and ipsec facilitate the configuration and management of firewalls and VPNs, securing network traffic and protecting sensitive data. By controlling access and encrypting communications, these tools help prevent unauthorized access and ensure data integrity and confidentiality.

Compatibility and Interoperability

Linux network commands are designed to be compatible with a wide range of network protocols and technologies, ensuring seamless integration with various systems and devices. This compatibility enhances interoperability, allowing Linux systems to communicate effectively with other platforms. Whether integrating with legacy systems or modern cloud environments, Linux network commands facilitate smooth and reliable interactions across diverse network infrastructures.

Automation and Scripting

One of the significant advantages of Linux network commands is their ability to be automated and scripted. Using scripting languages like Bash, Python, and Perl, administrators can automate repetitive network-related tasks, such as configuring interfaces and firewall rules. This automation reduces manual intervention, minimizes errors, and enhances overall efficiency. Custom scripts can also be developed to handle complex network management tasks, further streamlining operations.

Linux network commands are part of the open-source Linux operating system, which means they are freely available and continuously improved by a vibrant community of developers and administrators. This open-source nature allows for rapid development and enhancement of network tools, ensuring they remain up-to-date with the latest networking standards and technologies. Community contributions also foster innovation, enabling the introduction of new features and functionalities tailored to evolving network management needs.

Using 'ifconfig'

The ifconfig command is a fundamental utility in Linux used for configuring and managing network interface parameters. Despite being deprecated in favor of the more modern ip command, ifconfig remains widely used due to its simplicity and familiarity among system administrators. This command allows users to view and configure network interfaces, making it an essential tool for network management tasks.

Displaying Network Interfaces

To begin using ifconfig, open a terminal window. Simply typing ifconfig and pressing Enter will display a list of all network interfaces on your system along with their current configurations.

```
ifconfig
```

This command will output details for each network interface, including the interface name (e.g., eth0, wlan0), IP address, netmask, broadcast address, and other relevant settings.

Viewing Specific Interface Configuration

To view the configuration of a specific network interface, use the following syntax:

```
ifconfig <interface>
```

For example, to view the configuration of the eth0 interface, you would type:

```
ifconfig eth0
```

This command will display detailed information about the eth0 interface, such as its IP address, netmask, and broadcast address. This information is crucial for troubleshooting and verifying network settings.

Setting the IP Address

You can set the IP address of a network interface using the following syntax:

```
ifconfig <interface> <IP address>
```

For example, to set the IP address of the eth0 interface to 192.168.1.100, you would type:

```
ifconfig eth0 192.168.1.100
```

This command assigns the specified IP address to the eth0 interface, enabling it to communicate on the specified network.

Setting the Netmask

In addition to setting the IP address, you can also configure the netmask for a network interface using the following syntax:

```
ifconfig <interface> netmask <netmask>
```

For example, to set the netmask of the eth0 interface to 255.255.255.0, you would type:

```
ifconfig eth0 netmask 255.255.255.0
```

The netmask determines the network segment the interface belongs to, which is essential for proper network routing and communication.

Setting the Broadcast Address

The broadcast address can also be configured with ifconfig. The broadcast address allows communication with all devices on a network segment.

```
ifconfig <interface> broadcast <broadcast address>
```

For example, to set the broadcast address of the eth0 interface to 192.168.1.255, you would type:

```
ifconfig eth0 broadcast 192.168.1.255
```

Interface Up or Down

The ifconfig command can also be used to enable or disable a network interface. Bringing an interface up or down is useful for testing configurations or troubleshooting connectivity issues.

To bring an interface up:

```
ifconfig <interface> up
```

For example:

```
ifconfig eth0 up
```

To bring an interface down:

```
ifconfig <interface> down
```

For example:

```
ifconfig eth0 down
```

Additional Options

The ifconfig command also offers various additional options for advanced network configuration and troubleshooting:

Promiscuous Mode

Enabling promiscuous mode allows the interface to pass all traffic to the CPU, not just the packets addressed to it. This is useful for network debugging.

```
ifconfig eth0 promisc
```

MTU Size

You can change the Maximum Transmission Unit (MTU) size for an interface. The MTU defines the largest packet size that can be transmitted.

```
ifconfig eth0 mtu 1500
```

While newer tools like ip offer more advanced features and flexibility, ifconfig remains an essential part of the toolkit for many system administrators. Its usage enables efficient network configuration, troubleshooting, and management, ensuring that network interfaces operate optimally and securely.

Using 'iwconfig'

The iwconfig command is a specialized utility in Linux for configuring and managing wireless network interfaces. While ifconfig handles general network interface configurations, iwconfig is specifically designed for wireless settings, providing options to set the operating mode, frequency, SSID, and other parameters essential for wireless networking.

Displaying Wireless Interface Configuration

To begin using iwconfig, open a terminal window. Typing iwconfig and pressing Enter will display a list of your system's wireless interfaces along with their current configurations.

```
iwconfig
```

This command will output details for each wireless interface, including the interface name (e.g., wlan0), wireless mode, frequency, access point, bit rate, and other relevant settings.

Viewing Specific Wireless Interface Configuration

To view the configuration of a specific wireless interface, use the following syntax:

```
iwconfig <interface>
```

For example, to view the configuration of the wlan0 interface, you would type:

```
iwconfig wlan0
```

This command will display detailed information about the wlan0 interface, including its wireless mode, frequency, SSID, and signal quality. This information is crucial for troubleshooting and verifying wireless network settings.

Setting the Wireless Mode

You can set the wireless mode of an interface using the following syntax:

```
iwconfig <interface> mode <mode>
```

For example, to set the wireless mode of the wlan0 interface to managed, you would type:

```
iwconfig wlan0 mode managed
```

The managed mode is used when the wireless device connects to an access point. Other modes include ad-hoc, master, and monitor, each serving different networking scenarios.

Setting the Frequency or Channel

You can set the operating frequency or channel for a wireless interface using the following syntax:

```
iwconfig <interface> freq <frequency>
```

or

```
iwconfig <interface> channel <channel>
```

For example, to set the frequency of the wlan0 interface to 2.462GHz (which corresponds to channel 11), you would type:

```
iwconfig wlan0 freq 2.462G
```

Alternatively, to set it directly by channel:

```
iwconfig wlan0 channel 11
```

Setting the correct frequency or channel can help avoid interference and optimize wireless performance.

Setting the ESSID (Network Name)

You can set the ESSID (Extended Service Set Identifier), commonly known as the network name, using the following syntax:

```
iwconfig <interface> essid <network name>
```

For example, to connect the wlan0 interface to a network with the SSID MyNetwork, you would type:

```
iwconfig wlan0 essid MyNetwork
```

Setting the correct ESSID ensures that the wireless interface connects to the intended wireless network.

Setting the Network Key (WEP Key)

For networks that use WEP encryption, you can set the network key using the following syntax:

```
iwconfig <interface> key <key>
```

For example, to set the WEP key for the wlan0 interface, you would type:

```
iwconfig wlan0 key s:password123
```

In the above code snippet, s: indicates that the key is an ASCII string. Properly setting the network key is essential for securing wireless communications.

Setting the Bit Rate

You can set the bit rate of the wireless interface to optimize performance using the following syntax:

```
iwconfig <interface> rate <bit rate>
```

For example, to set the bit rate of the wlan0 interface to 54Mb/s, you would type:

```
iwconfig wlan0 rate 54M
```

Setting the bit rate appropriately can improve the quality and speed of the wireless connection.

Monitor Mode

Monitor mode allows a wireless interface to capture all packets on the wireless network, which is useful for network analysis and security assessments.

```
iwconfig <interface> mode monitor
```

For example:

```
iwconfig wlan0 mode monitor
```

Monitor mode is particularly useful for network debugging and security testing, as it allows administrators to capture and analyze all wireless traffic. The iwconfig command also provides various additional options for advanced wireless configuration and troubleshooting:

- Tx-Power

Adjust the transmission power of the wireless interface to control the range and power consumption.

```
iwconfig wlan0 txpower 20
```

- Sensitivity

Set the sensitivity threshold for the wireless interface.

```
iwconfig wlan0 sens -80
```

Using the iwconfig command, administrators may fine-tune wireless performance, bolster communication security, and fix connectivity problems. When you use iwconfig, you can control your wireless networks efficiently and effectively, guaranteeing that your wireless connections are dependable and of excellent quality.

Using 'dig'

The dig command is a powerful tool for querying the Domain Name System (DNS) in Linux. It is used to perform DNS lookups and provides detailed information about DNS records, making it an invaluable tool for network administrators and developers for troubleshooting DNS issues and verifying DNS configurations.

Basic DNS Lookup

To begin using dig, open a terminal window. Typing dig followed by the domain name you want to look up and pressing Enter will perform a basic DNS query.

```
dig gitforgits.com
```

This command will return detailed information about the DNS records for the domain gitforgits.com, including the IP address associated with it.

Performing a Reverse DNS Lookup

A reverse DNS lookup maps an IP address to a domain name. To perform a reverse DNS lookup, use the -x option followed by the IP address.

```
dig -x <IP address>
```

For example, to perform a reverse DNS lookup for the IP address 192.0.2.1, you would type:

```
dig -x 192.0.2.1
```

This will return the domain name associated with the IP address 192.0.2.1.

Specifying a DNS Server

You can specify which DNS server to use for the query by including the server's address after the domain name, prefixed with the @ symbol.

```
dig <domain> @<server>
```

For example, to perform a DNS lookup for the domain gitforgits.com using Google's public DNS server 8.8.8.8, you would type:

```
dig gitforgits.com @8.8.8.8
```

This directs the query to the specified DNS server, which can be useful for troubleshooting DNS propagation or testing responses from different DNS servers.

Querying Specific DNS Records

The dig command can be used to query specific types of DNS records, such as A, MX, CNAME, TXT, and others. To specify the record type, include it before the domain name.

```
dig <record type> <domain>
```

For example, to query the MX (Mail Exchange) records for gitforgits.com, you would type:

```
dig MX gitforgits.com
```

This will return the mail servers responsible for receiving email for the domain. The dig command also offers a variety of options for more detailed and customized queries:

- +short

Displays a concise output of the query results.

```
dig gitforgits.com +short
```

- +trace

Traces the entire path taken by the query from the root servers to the authoritative servers for the domain.

```
dig gitforgits.com +trace
```

- +stats

Includes statistics about the query, such as query time and server information.

```
dig gitforgits.com +stats
```

When taken as a whole, Dig offers broad insights into DNS setups, which makes it possible to efficiently diagnose and verify DNS records.

Using 'traceroute'

The traceroute command is a network diagnostic tool used to trace the path that packets take from the source system to a specified destination. It provides information about each hop along the route, including the round-trip time (RTT) for each hop, which is useful for identifying network bottlenecks and routing issues.

Basic Tracing

To begin using traceroute, open a terminal window. Typing traceroute followed by the domain name or IP address of the destination and pressing Enter will display the path taken by packets to reach the destination.

```
traceroute gitforgits.com
```

This command will display a list of hops taken by the packets to reach gitforgits.com, along with the RTT for each hop.

Specifying Maximum Hops

You can limit the maximum number of hops to trace by using the -m option.

```
traceroute -m <hops> <destination>
```

For example, to trace the path to gitforgits.com with a maximum of 10 hops, you would type:

```
traceroute -m 10 gitforgits.com
```

This can be useful for limiting the scope of the trace in large networks.

Specifying a Port Number

You can specify the port number to use for the trace using the -p option. This is particularly useful for tracing the path to services running on non-standard ports.

```
traceroute -p <port> <destination>
```

For example, to trace the path to gitforgits.com using port 80, you would type:

```
traceroute -p 80 gitforgits.com
```

Additional Options

The traceroute command offers several additional options for customized tracing:

- -n

Displays numeric IP addresses instead of resolving hostnames, which can speed up the trace.

```
traceroute -n gitforgits.com
```

- -I

Uses ICMP Echo instead of UDP packets.

```
traceroute -I gitforgits.com
```

- -T

Uses TCP SYN packets instead of UDP packets.

```
traceroute -T gitforgits.com
```

From this point forward, Traceroute is able to successfully trace the path that packets follow throughout a network, thereby revealing bottlenecks and routing faults that can have an impact on the performance of the network.

Using 'netstat'

The netstat command is a versatile tool in Linux for displaying information about active network connections, routing tables, interface statistics, masquerade connections, and multicast memberships. It is essential for network troubleshooting and performance monitoring.

Displaying Active Network Connections

To begin using netstat, open a terminal window. Typing netstat and pressing Enter will display a list of active network connections, along with their state, local and remote addresses, and the process ID (PID) of the program associated with each connection.

```
netstat
```

This command provides a comprehensive overview of the current network activity on your system.

Displaying All Active Connections

To include all active connections, including those in the listening state, use the -a option:

```
netstat -a
```

This option is useful for identifying services that are waiting for incoming connections.

Filtering by Protocol

You can filter the connections displayed by netstat to show only those for a specific protocol using the -p option followed by the protocol name.

```
netstat -p <protocol>
```

For example, to display only the TCP connections, you would type:

```
netstat -p tcp
```

This is particularly useful for monitoring specific types of network traffic.

Displaying Kernel Routing Table

To view the kernel routing table, use the -r option:

```
netstat -r
```

This command displays the routing table, showing how packets are routed through the network. It includes information such as the destination network, gateway, and interface used for each route.

The netstat command offers a variety of options for more detailed and specific information:

- -i

Display network interface statistics.

```
netstat -i
```

- -g

Display multicast group membership information.

```
netstat -g
```

- -s

Display summary statistics for each protocol.

```
netstat -s
```

- -c

Continuously display updated network statistics.

```
netstat -c
```

To better manage and troubleshoot networks, the netstat gives precise information about active connections, routing tables, and interface data. When you know your way around netstat, you can keep an eye on your network's performance, identify problems, and make sure everything runs smoothly.

Using 'nslookup'

The nslookup command is a useful tool for querying the Domain Name System (DNS) in Linux. It allows users to retrieve information about domain names and IP addresses, making it essential for diagnosing DNS issues and verifying DNS configurations.

Performing a Basic DNS Lookup

To begin using nslookup, open a terminal window. Typing nslookup followed by the domain name you want to look up and pressing Enter will perform a basic DNS query.

```
nslookup gitforgits.com
```

This command will return the IP address associated with the domain name gitforgits.com, along with additional DNS information such as the authoritative DNS server.

Performing a Reverse DNS Lookup

A reverse DNS lookup maps an IP address to a domain name. To perform a reverse DNS lookup, use the following syntax:

```
nslookup <IP address>
```

For example, to perform a reverse DNS lookup for the IP address 192.0.2.1, you would type:

```
nslookup 192.0.2.1
```

This will return the domain name associated with the IP address 192.0.2.1.

Specifying a DNS Server

You can specify which DNS server to use for the query by entering the server command followed by the server's address. This is useful for testing and troubleshooting DNS issues from different DNS servers.

```
nslookup

> server <server>

> <domain>
```

For example, to perform a DNS lookup for the domain gitforgits.com using Google's public DNS server 8.8.8.8, you would type:

```
nslookup

> server 8.8.8.8

> gitforgits.com
```

This directs the query to the specified DNS server, which can help identify discrepancies or issues with specific DNS servers.

Querying Specific DNS Records

The nslookup command can also be used to query specific types of DNS records, such as A, MX, CNAME, and others. To specify the record type, use the set command before the domain name.

```
nslookup

> set type=<record type>
```

```
> <domain>
```

For example, to query the MX (Mail Exchange) records for gitforgits.com, you would type:

```
nslookup

> set type=MX

> gitforgits.com
```

This command will return the mail servers responsible for handling email for the domain.

Interactive Mode

nslookup also supports an interactive mode, where you can enter multiple commands in a single session. To enter interactive mode, simply type nslookup and press Enter. You can then type commands one by one.

```
nslookup
```

Once in interactive mode, you can set various options and perform multiple queries without exiting the tool. For example:

```
> server 8.8.8.8

> gitforgits.com

> set type=MX

> gitforgits.com

> exit
```

The nslookup command offers several additional options for more detailed and customized queries:

- set debug

Provides detailed debugging information for each query.

```
nslookup
```

```
> set debug

> gitforgits.com
```

- set port=<port number>

Specifies the port number to use for the DNS query, which is useful for testing non-standard DNS server configurations. nslookup

```
> set port=5353

> gitforgits.com
```

- set timeout=<seconds>

Sets the timeout interval for waiting for a reply. This can be useful for slow or unreliable network connections. nslookup

```
> set timeout=10

> gitforgits.com
```

In general, the nslookup command helps with DNS verification and troubleshooting by providing detailed information about IP addresses and domain names.

Searching Wireless Devices

Searching for wireless devices involves detecting and recognizing wireless networks that are in proximity to your device. This process is valuable for establishing a wireless connection or collecting data on available wireless networks in a specific area. Linux provides the iwlist command, which enables users to scan for wireless networks. This command provides comprehensive details about the wireless interfaces installed on your system and the available wireless networks.

Preparing Wireless Interface

Before utilizing the iwlist command, ensure that your wireless interface is operational. You can verify the status of your wireless interface using the ifconfig command. If the interface is inactive, you can activate it with the following command:

```
ifconfig <interface> up
```

Replace <interface> with the name of your wireless interface, such as wlan0.

```
ifconfig wlan0 up
```

Alternatively, using the ip command:

```
ip link set wlan0 up
```

Scanning for Wireless Networks

To search for wireless devices, scan for wireless networks using the iwlist command as below:

```
iwlist <interface> scan
```

Replace <interface> with the name of your wireless interface, such as wlan0.

```
iwlist wlan0 scan
```

This command will scan for wireless networks in range and display a list of the available networks, including their SSID (network name), frequency, signal strength, and encryption type.

Connecting to a Wireless Network

Once you have identified the wireless network you want to connect to, you can use the iwconfig command to establish the connection as below:

```
iwconfig <interface> essid <SSID> key <key>
```

Replace <interface> with the name of your wireless interface (e.g., wlan0), <SSID> with the network name of the wireless network you want to connect to, and <key> with the network key (password).

For example, to connect to a wireless network with the SSID MyNetwork and the key password123, you would type:

```
iwconfig wlan0 essid MyNetwork key password123
```

Verifying Connection

After connecting to the wireless network, you can verify the connection by using the iwconfig command again. The output should show that the wireless interface is associated with the SSID of the network you are connected to.

```
iwconfig wlan0
```

The output will confirm the connection details, including the ESSID, frequency, and signal level.

The iwlist command offers additional options for more detailed scanning and network information:

- Scanning Specific Frequencies

You can scan specific frequencies by specifying the frequency range.

```
iwlist wlan0 freq
```

- Detailed Scanning Information

The iwlist command can provide detailed information about each network, including the encryption method, supported bit rates, and more.

```
iwlist wlan0 scan | less
```

If you know your way around getting your wireless interface ready, scanning for networks, and connecting to them, you'll be a master of wireless connectivity management. When combined with iwlist and iwconfig, you'll be able to fix wireless problems, fix network performance, and guarantee dependable wireless connections.

Modifying IPv4 Addresses

Understanding IPv4

An IPv4 address is a unique numerical label assigned to each device on a computer network that uses the Internet Protocol for communication. It is a 32-bit number divided into four octets separated by periods, with each octet represented by an 8-bit number, allowing values between 0 and 255.

IPv4 addresses consist of two main parts: the network prefix and the host identifier. The network prefix identifies the network to which the device is connected, while the host identifier specifies the device within that network. The division between the network prefix and host identifier is determined by the subnet mask.

Hierarchical Structure

IPv4 addresses follow a hierarchical structure, enabling devices on different networks to communicate through routers. When a device sends a packet to another device on a different network, routers forward the packet based on the network prefix until it reaches the destination network.

Subnet Mask

The subnet mask is a 32-bit number consisting of a series of contiguous 1s followed by a series of contiguous 0s. The 1s represent the network prefix, and the 0s represent the host identifier. By performing a logical AND operation between an IP address and the subnet mask, you can determine the network prefix.

IPv4 Limitations

The IPv4 address space provides approximately 4.3 billion unique addresses. However, the rapid growth of devices connected to the internet has made this address space insufficient, leading to the development of IPv6 addresses. IPv6 addresses are 128-bit numbers, represented in hexadecimal notation, providing a vastly larger address space.

Despite the introduction of IPv6, IPv4 remains widely used due to the extensive infrastructure already in place and the gradual transition process.

Modifying IPv4 Addresses

To modify the IPv4 address of a network interface in Linux, you can use the ifconfig or ip command. Following are the detailed steps for using both commands.

Using ifconfig

- Setting the IP Address

```
ifconfig eth0 192.168.1.100
```

This command assigns the IP address 192.168.1.100 to the eth0 interface.

- Setting the netmask

```
ifconfig eth0 netmask 255.255.255.0
```

This command sets the netmask for the eth0 interface to 255.255.255.0.

- Setting the broadcast address

```
ifconfig eth0 broadcast 192.168.1.255
```

This command sets the broadcast address for the eth0 interface to 192.168.1.255.

Using ip

The ip command offers more flexibility and additional features compared to ifconfig. Here's how to use it:

- Adding an IP address

```
ip addr add 192.168.1.100/24 dev eth0
```

This command adds the IP address 192.168.1.100 with a netmask of 255.255.255.0 (indicated by /24) to the eth0 interface.

- Setting the default route

```
ip route add default via 192.168.1.1 dev eth0
```

This command sets the default route for the eth0 interface through the gateway 192.168.1.1.

- Deleting an IP address

```
ip addr del 192.168.1.100/24 dev eth0
```

This command deletes the IP address 192.168.1.100 from the eth0 interface.

Modifying IPv6 Addresses

Modifying IPv6 addresses on a Linux system can be done using either the ifconfig or ip command. The process is straightforward and involves deleting the existing IPv6 address and adding a new one.

Below are detailed steps and examples for both commands:

Using ifconfig

The ifconfig command can be used to manage IPv6 addresses, although it is less commonly used than the ip command for this purpose. Given below is how you can modify IPv6 addresses using ifconfig:

- Delete the existing IPv6 address

```
ifconfig eth0 inet6 del 2001:db8:0:1::10/64
```

This command removes the IPv6 address 2001:db8:0:1::10/64 from the eth0 interface.

- Add the new IPv6 address

```
ifconfig eth0 inet6 add 2001:db8:0:1::20/64
```

This command assigns the new IPv6 address 2001:db8:0:1::20/64 to the eth0 interface.

Using ip

The ip command is more flexible and powerful for managing network interfaces and addresses. It is the preferred method for configuring IPv6 addresses. Given below is how you can modify IPv6 addresses using the ip command:

- Delete the existing IPv6 address and add the new one

```
ip -6 addr replace 2001:db8:0:1::20/64 dev eth0
```

This single command replaces the existing IPv6 address with the new one on the eth0 interface.

- Test connectivity with the new IPv6 address

```
ping6 2001:db8:0:1::20
```

This command sends ICMP echo requests to the new IPv6 address to verify that it is correctly configured and reachable. A successful ping response indicates that the new IPv6 address has been set correctly.

Deleting IP Address

Managing network configurations often involves not only adding or modifying IP addresses but also removing them when they are no longer needed. Both ifconfig and ip commands can be used to delete IP addresses from network interfaces in Linux.

Below are the steps and examples for deleting IPv6 addresses using these commands:

45

Using ifconfig

The ifconfig command can be used to delete an IPv6 address from a network interface. Given below is the syntax and an example:

- Delete the existing IPv6 address

```
ifconfig <interface> inet6 del <IPv6 address>
```

Replace <interface> with the name of the network interface (e.g., eth0) and <IPv6 address> with the IPv6 address you want to delete (e.g., 2001:db8:0:1::1/64).

For example, to delete the IPv6 address 2001:db8:0:1::1/64 from the eth0 interface, you would type:

```
ifconfig eth0 inet6 del 2001:db8:0:1::1/64
```

Using ip

The ip command is the preferred method for managing network configurations, including deleting IP addresses. Given below is the syntax and an example:

- Delete the existing IPv6 address

```
ip -6 addr del <IPv6 address> dev <interface>
```

Replace <IPv6 address> with the IPv6 address you want to delete (e.g., 2001:db8:0:1::1/64) and <interface> with the name of the network interface (e.g., eth0).

For example, to delete the IPv6 address 2001:db8:0:1::1/64 from the eth0 interface, you would type:

```
ip -6 addr del 2001:db8:0:1::1/64 dev eth0
```

Cloning IP Addresses

What is IP Address Cloning?

IP address cloning refers to the process of assigning a device multiple IP addresses associated with different network interfaces. This technique can be employed for various purposes, such as allowing a device to communicate with multiple networks simultaneously or bypassing IP address restrictions. Cloning an IP address can be done through virtual network interfaces, network address translation (NAT), or proxy servers to route traffic between the device and multiple networks.

However, cloning an IP address must be handled with caution as it can potentially violate network policies and cause conflicts or security issues. It is often recommended to use alternative methods like NAT or virtual network interfaces to achieve the desired network configuration.

Steps to Clone an IP Address

The following steps outline a general approach to cloning an IP address on a Linux system.

1. Determine the IP address to clone and the network interface to use.

2. Ensure the operating system and network architecture support IP address cloning. Some systems may require virtual network interfaces or NAT to achieve the same effect.

3. Modify the network settings or add the IP address to the interface using command-line tools.

4. Verify that the cloned IP address works as intended by pinging other devices or connecting to networks using the cloned IP address.

5. Keep an eye out for any issues or conflicts that may arise from the IP address cloning.

Note: These above outlined steps may vary depending on the operating system and network architecture.

Sample Program: Cloning an IP Address

Following is a sample program to clone an IP address on a Linux machine using a virtual network interface:

Suppose you want to clone the IP address 192.168.1.100 on the eth0 interface. First, create a virtual network interface:

```
ip link add link eth0 name eth0:1 type macvlan
```

This command creates a virtual network interface named eth0:1 linked to the eth0 interface.

Then, assign the IP address to the virtual network interface:

```
ifconfig eth0:1 192.168.1.100
```

This assigns the IP address 192.168.1.100 to the virtual network interface eth0:1.

Ping other devices on the network or attempt to connect to other networks using the cloned IP address to ensure it is functioning as intended.

After this, keep track of any issues or conflicts that arise as a result of the IP address cloning.

Points to Remember

When cloning an IP address, it's important to consider several factors to ensure a smooth process and avoid potential issues.

- Ensure that the IP address you want to clone is not already in use on the network. Using an IP address already assigned to another device can cause conflicts and connectivity issues.

- Consult with your network administrator or IT department to ensure that IP address cloning is allowed on your network. Some networks have strict policies regarding IP address assignment.

- Cloning an IP address can complicate network activity tracking and may provide an easier entry point for attackers. Weigh the risks and benefits before proceeding with IP address cloning.

- After cloning an IP address, monitor the network for any connectivity issues or conflicts. Be prepared to modify the network settings or disable the cloned IP address if problems arise.

A few situations call for IP address cloning, and those include load balancing and network testing. To prevent security breaches and network interruptions, it should be handled with care.

Evaluating DNS Server

Need for DNS Evaluation

Evaluating DNS records and DNS server performance is crucial for several reasons:

- Troubleshooting Connectivity Issues: DNS problems can often lead to connectivity issues. By evaluating DNS records, you can identify misconfigurations or errors that might be causing these problems. Analyzing these records helps pinpoint the root cause and facilitates a solution.

- Identifying Security Risks: DNS records can expose sensitive information such as server IP addresses and domain locations. Evaluating these records can uncover unauthorized or malicious changes, helping to prevent potential security breaches.

- Optimizing Performance: Checking DNS records ensures that your website or network uses a fast and reliable DNS provider. Regular evaluation helps monitor DNS infrastructure performance and identify bottlenecks, ensuring optimal network performance.

- Ensuring Compliance: Organizations often have strict policies regarding DNS usage. Regular DNS evaluation ensures adherence to these policies and compliance with regulations, safeguarding against policy violations.

Steps to Evaluate DNS Server

Evaluating a DNS server involves several steps to ensure optimal performance, security, and compliance. Following is a detailed step-by-step walkthrough:

Identify the DNS Server

Determine the DNS server you want to evaluate. Use command-line tools like nslookup or dig to look up DNS records for a domain or hostname, or use web-based DNS lookup tools.

Test DNS Server Performance

Measure the time taken by the DNS server to resolve a domain or hostname using tools like dig or nslookup.

```
dig gitforgits.com

nslookup gitforgits.com
```

For more comprehensive performance testing under different workloads, use tools like dnsperf or resperf.

```
dnsperf -s <DNS server> -d queryfile

resperf -s <DNS server> -d queryfile
```

Check DNS Server Security

DNS servers are common targets for cyberattacks. Use tools like dnssec-tools or dnssec-analyze to check security settings and configurations.

```
dnssec-tools <options>

dnssec-analyze gitforgits.com
```

Test the server's SSL/TLS security using tools like sslyze.

```
sslyze --regular <DNS server>
```

Ensure Compliance

If you need to adhere to specific policies or regulations, use tools like dnssec-policy or dnssec-compliance to ensure the DNS server meets regulatory requirements.

```
dnssec-policy -c <config_file>
```

```
dnssec-compliance gitforgits.com
```

Monitor the DNS Server

Regular monitoring helps identify issues before they become major problems. Use tools like dns-monitor or dnstap for continuous monitoring.

```
dns-monitor <options>
```

```
dnstap -c <config_file>
```

Administrators can improve security, optimize performance, discover and resolve issues, and maintain regulatory compliance by following the above outlined systematic strategy and employing appropriate tools. To keep a network infrastructure strong and efficient, it is also essential to evaluate and monitor DNS regularly.

Modifying DNS Server

Approach to Modify DNS Server

Modifying a DNS server involves careful planning and execution to ensure continued optimal functionality. Depending on the network architecture and operating system, various methods can be employed to modify DNS servers.

Following are the general steps to follow when you need to modify a DNS server.

1. Determine the specific DNS server you want to modify. This could be a local DNS server on your network, a remote DNS server provided by your ISP, or a third-party DNS provider.

2. Identify the settings or configurations you want to change. This may include the IP address of the DNS server, the DNS records it maintains, or the security settings for the server.

3. Access the DNS server's configuration interface. This can be done using a web-based interface, a command-line tool, or by editing configuration files directly on the server. The method you use will depend on the specific DNS server and network architecture.

4. Modify the DNS server settings as required. This could involve changing the IP address, adding or removing DNS records, or updating security settings. Ensure that any changes made are accurate to avoid connectivity issues or other problems.

5. After making the modifications, save the changes and test the DNS server to ensure it is working correctly. You can use tools like ping, dig, or nslookup to verify the server's functionality.

6. Always create a backup of the DNS server's configuration before making any changes. In case of issues, you can restore the previous configuration to maintain the server's operation. Document the changes made for future reference and troubleshooting.

Sample Program: Modifying DNS Server

To begin with, at first, determine whether the DNS server is local, remote, or provided by a third party. Then, decide if you need to update the IP address, modify DNS records, or change security settings.

For a web-based interface, navigate to the DNS server's management portal. And, for command-line tools, use SSH to access the server:

```
ssh user@dnsserver
```

Change the IP Address:

```
vim /etc/resolv.conf
```

Update the nameserver entries with the new IP addresses. And then edit the zone files directly:

```
vim /etc/bind/db.gitforgits.com
```

Add or remove A, CNAME, MX, etc., records as needed. And, modify DNSSEC settings or access control lists (ACLs) in the configuration files.

Then, save and test the changes by restarting the DNS service as below.

```
systemctl restart bind9
```

Or

```
service named restart

dig gitforgits.com

nslookup gitforgits.com
```

Test the connectivity:

```
ping -c 4 dnsserver
```

Finding the server, gaining access to its configuration interface, making exact alterations, and finally, testing the changes properly are all steps in the multi-step process of fixing a DNS server. If you want to keep the DNS server up and running and fix any problems fast, you must also create backups and record the changes.

Summary

Throughout this chapter, we have explored the significance of Linux in the realm of networking. We have analyzed the key characteristics of Linux, such as its open-source nature, flexibility, and security features. We have also covered its capacity to support multiple network interfaces, virtualization, containerization, and various networking protocols. Furthermore, we have emphasized the importance of networking commands in Linux, which facilitate network administrators in configuring, monitoring, and resolving network connectivity issues. Among the essential networking commands in Linux are ifconfig, ping, netstat, nslookup, traceroute, tcpdump, iptables, route, and ip.

We have also highlighted the crucial role that network services play in managing and maintaining network infrastructure. In Linux, network services such as DNS, DHCP, web servers, email servers, and database servers are vital, and Linux provides powerful tools for configuring and managing these services. Lastly, we have emphasized the significance of network management tools and utilities in Linux. These tools allow network administrators to manage and maintain network infrastructure, analyze network performance, and ensure the availability and reliability of network resources.

CHAPTER 3: RUST BASICS FOR NETWORKS

Overview

Rust is a programming language with immense potential in the field of networking. As a low-level language, it can produce highly efficient code, enabling faster and more reliable network communications. Designed as a general-purpose language, Rust is suitable for a wide range of networking applications, from simple client-server models to complex distributed systems.

Robust Memory and Data Safety

One of Rust's key strengths lies in its robust memory and data safety guarantees. Rust's ownership system and strict compile-time checks help prevent common errors such as buffer overflows and null pointer dereferences, which are often the culprits behind network security vulnerabilities. By ensuring memory safety without the need for a garbage collector, Rust minimizes runtime overhead and maximizes performance. This is particularly beneficial in networking, where efficient memory management is crucial for handling high volumes of data and connections.

Rust's static typing system also plays a critical role in ensuring data integrity. By defining the types of data being transmitted at compile time, Rust reduces the risk of data corruption and security breaches. This level of type safety helps developers catch errors early in the development process, leading to more robust and reliable network applications.

Asynchronous Programming and Concurrency

Modern networking often requires handling multiple connections and data streams simultaneously. Rust excels in this area with its strong support for asynchronous programming. The async/await syntax allows developers to write non-blocking code that can handle many tasks concurrently, improving overall network performance and reducing latency.

Asynchronous programming is powered by the Tokio runtime, which provides a reliable and scalable foundation for building networked applications. With Tokio, developers can create applications that efficiently manage thousands of simultaneous connections, making Rust an excellent choice for high-performance network servers and real-time communication systems.

Tools for Debugging and Profiling

Rust offers powerful tools for debugging and profiling, which are essential for developing high-quality network applications. Tools like cargo, Rust's package manager and build system, streamline the development process by managing dependencies and building projects efficiently. For debugging, Rust integrates well with tools like GDB and LLDB, providing robust support for diagnosing issues in network code.

Profiling tools, such as perf and flamegraph, help developers identify performance bottlenecks and optimize their applications. These tools are invaluable for ensuring that network applications run smoothly and efficiently, even under heavy load.

Community and Ecosystem

Rust's growing community is another significant advantage. The Rust community is known for its inclusivity and focus on constructive collaboration, providing a supportive environment for developers of all experience levels. This community-driven approach has led to the development of numerous libraries and frameworks that simplify network programming.

The Rust ecosystem includes a variety of crates (libraries are generally termed as crates in Rust) that facilitate networking tasks. For example, the hyper crate is widely used for building HTTP clients and servers, while the reqwest crate provides a high-level HTTP client for easy integration with web services. These libraries, combined with Rust's inherent strengths, make it a powerful tool for network programming.

Variables

A variable refers to a term that points to a value stored in memory. Variables in Rust come with several unique features and behaviors that set them apart from those in other programming languages.

Default Immutability

By default, variables in Rust are immutable. Once a value is bound to a variable, it cannot be changed. This immutability ensures safety and predictability in your programs, preventing accidental modifications of data. Given below is an example of declaring and assigning a value to an immutable variable:

```
let x = 5;
```

Creating Mutable Variables

If you need to change the value of a variable after its initial assignment, you must explicitly declare it as mutable using the mut keyword. This tells the Rust compiler that the variable's value can be altered.

```
let mut y = 10;

y = 20; // Now y holds the value 20
```

Declaring Variables without Initial Values

Rust also allows you to declare a variable without assigning an initial value. However, if the variable is meant to be mutable and you plan to assign a value later, you must use the mut keyword.

```
let mut z;

z = 15;
```

Specifying Variable Types

Although Rust often infers the type of a variable, specifying the type explicitly is considered good practice. This helps the compiler catch type-related errors at compile time and makes the code more readable.

```
let a: i32 = 20;

let mut b: f64 = 3.14;
```

Shadowing Variables

Shadowing is a feature that allows you to declare a new variable with the same name as an existing variable. The new variable shadows the previous one, and its scope is limited to the block where it is declared. Shadowing can be used to change the type or mutability of a variable or to temporarily change its value.

Changing Type/Mutability

You can shadow a variable to change its type or make it mutable. Following is an example where the type of x is changed from i32 to f64:

```
let x = 5;

let x: f64 = x as f64;
```

In the above code snippet, the x variable is first declared as an i32 with the value 5. Then, it is shadowed by a new x variable of type f64.

Temporarily Changing Values

Shadowing can also be used to temporarily change the value of a variable without affecting the original value. For instance:

```
let x = 10;
```

```
let x = 5; // Shadowing x with a new value
```

In this case, the original x with the value 10 is shadowed by a new x with the value 5. After the scope of the shadowing ends, the original value of x is retained.

Sample Program: Using Immutable and Mutable Variables

Given below is a sample program demonstrating the use of immutable and mutable variables, specifying types, and shadowing:

```
fn main() {

    // Immutable variable

    let a = 10;

    println!("The value of a is: {}", a);


    // Mutable variable

    let mut b = 20;

    println!("The initial value of b is: {}", b);

    b = 30;

    println!("The new value of b is: {}", b);


    // Specifying variable type

    let c: i64 = 40;

    println!("The value of c is: {}", c);


    // Shadowing variable to change type
```

```
let d = 2.5; // f64 by default

let d: i32 = d as i32;

println!("The value of d after shadowing is: {}", d);


// Shadowing variable to change value temporarily

let e = 50;

{

    let e = 5;

    println!("The value of e inside block is: {}",
e);

}

println!("The value of e outside block is: {}", e);

}
```

In the above given example, variables a, b, c, d, and e showcase different aspects of variable declaration, mutability, type specification, and shadowing. This approach ensures efficient and secure handling of data and also leverages Rust's strong compile-time guarantees to minimize runtime errors.

Constants

A constant is a variable type that cannot be changed once it is defined. Constants are declared using the const keyword and must always be initialized with a value. Unlike variables declared with let, constants cannot be made mutable and their values are bound to remain unchanged throughout the program's execution. This immutability makes constants especially useful in scenarios where a value is used multiple times and must remain consistent, such as in networking programs.

Declaring Constants

Constants are declared with the const keyword followed by the constant name, type annotation, and value. The convention is to use uppercase letters for constant names with underscores separating words.

```
const MAX_CONNECTIONS: u32 = 100;
```

This declares a constant named MAX_CONNECTIONS with a value of 100. The type annotation u32 indicates that the value is an unsigned 32-bit integer.

In a networking context, constants can be used to store values like maximum number of connections, default ports, timeout durations, and more. Using constants ensures that these important values remain consistent and unchanged throughout the program.

Given below is an example of using a constant in a function that checks if the number of connections exceeds the allowed maximum:

```
const MAX_CONNECTIONS: u32 = 100;


fn accept_connections(num_connections: u32) {

    if num_connections > MAX_CONNECTIONS {

        println!("Too many connections, maximum allowed
is {}", MAX_CONNECTIONS);

    } else {

        println!("Connections accepted");

    }

}


fn main() {

    let current_connections = 80;

    accept_connections(current_connections);
```

```
    let current_connections = 120;

    accept_connections(current_connections);

}
```

In this example, the MAX_CONNECTIONS constant is used to ensure that the maximum number of connections remains consistent. The accept_connections function uses this constant to compare the current number of connections and print an appropriate message.

Sample Program: Using Constants to Handle Port Numbers and Buffer Sizes

Let us take a much more detailed example where constants are used in a networking context to handle configurations such as port numbers and buffer sizes.

```
const MAX_CONNECTIONS: u32 = 100;

const SERVER_PORT: u16 = 8080;

const BUFFER_SIZE: usize = 4096;


fn start_server() {

    println!("Starting server on port {}", SERVER_PORT);

    // Server initialization code...

}


fn accept_connections(num_connections: u32) {

    if num_connections > MAX_CONNECTIONS {
```

```rust
        println!("Too many connections, maximum allowed
is {}", MAX_CONNECTIONS);
    } else {
        println!("Connections accepted");
    }
}


fn read_data(buffer: &mut [u8]) {
    println!("Reading data into buffer of size {}",
BUFFER_SIZE);
    // Data reading code...
}


fn main() {
    start_server();

    let current_connections = 80;
    accept_connections(current_connections);


    let current_connections = 120;
    accept_connections(current_connections);
```

```
    let mut buffer = [0u8; BUFFER_SIZE];

    read_data(&mut buffer);

}
```

In the above given example,

- MAX_CONNECTIONS ensures the server does not accept more than the allowed number of connections.
- SERVER_PORT sets the port number for the server, ensuring all network operations refer to the same port.
- BUFFER_SIZE sets the size of the buffer used for reading data, ensuring consistency in buffer handling.

By defining constants, you ensure that these values are used correctly and consistently, improving the readability, maintainability, and overall robustness of your code.

Functions

One of the most important ways to create reusable code is to use functions. Code readability and maintainability are both improvised by their use, as is the code's organization into smaller, more manageable modules. A function's body can hold numerous statements, accept different kinds of parameters, and return values.

Defining a Function

A function is defined using the fn keyword, followed by the function name, a list of parameters, and the return type. The function body is enclosed in curly braces {}.

Following is a simple example of a function definition:

```
fn greet(name: &str) -> String {

    format!("Hello, {}!", name)

}


fn main() {
```

```rust
    let greeting = greet("Alice");

    println!("{}", greeting);

}
```

In the above code snippet, the greet function takes a string slice name as an argument and returns a String. The format! macro is used to create a new String with the greeting message.

Sample Program: Validating an IP Address

In a networking context, functions are particularly useful for tasks such as validating IP addresses, processing data packets, or managing connections. Following is an example of a function that validates an IPv4 address:

```rust
fn is_valid_ip(ip_address: &str) -> bool {

    let octets: Vec<&str> =
ip_address.split('.').collect();


    if octets.len() != 4 {

        return false;

    }


    for octet in octets {

        match octet.parse::<u8>() {

            Ok(num) => {

                if num > 255 {

                    return false;

                }
```

```rust
        },
        Err(_) => {

            return false;

        }

    }

}


    true

}


fn main() {

    let ip1 = "192.168.1.1";

    let ip2 = "256.256.256.256";


    println!("Is {} a valid IP? {}", ip1,
is_valid_ip(ip1)); // true

    println!("Is {} a valid IP? {}", ip2,
is_valid_ip(ip2)); // false

}
```

This function, is_valid_ip, takes a string slice ip_address as its argument and returns a boolean indicating whether the IP address is valid.

In the above program,

- The IP address string is split by the . character and the resulting substrings are collected into a vector called octets.

- The function checks if the length of the octets vector is 4. If not, it returns false.

- The function iterates over each octet in the octets vector, attempting to parse it as a u8 integer. If the parse is successful and the resulting number is between 0 and 255, the function continues. Otherwise, it returns false.

- If all octets are successfully parsed and valid, the function returns true.

Advanced Function Features

Rust also supports advanced features in functions such as:

- Closures: Anonymous functions that can capture variables from their environment.

- Generics: Functions that can operate on different data types.

- Higher-Order Functions: Functions that take other functions as arguments or return them as results.

Following is an example of a closure that checks if a number is even:

```
fn main() {

    let is_even = |num: i32| -> bool {

        num % 2 == 0

    };


    let number = 4;

    println!("Is {} even? {}", number, is_even(number));
// true

}
```

In the above code snippet, is_even is a closure that takes an integer and returns a boolean indicating whether the number is even. Functions enhance the modularity, readability, and maintainability of your networking applications especially in processing data, managing connections, and performing validations, such as checking the validity of IP addresses.

Control Flow

Overview

Control flow refers to the order in which instructions in a program are executed. It determines the path a program takes through its code and how it responds to different conditions and inputs. In networking, especially while using rust, control flow is crucial for managing the flow of data between networked devices, handling errors and exceptions, and ensuring that programs are responsive and scalable. One of the key control flow structures in Rust networking is the event loop.

An event loop is a program construct that waits for events to occur, such as incoming data from a network socket, and then responds to those events. Event loops are typically implemented using the Tokio runtime, which is an asynchronous, non-blocking I/O framework.

The Tokio runtime provides core abstractions such as futures, streams, and sinks, which represent asynchronous operations and data flows. These abstractions, combined with the event loop, create a powerful and flexible programming model for Rust networking.

Sample Program: Implementing Event Loop using Tokio

At a high level, the structure of a Tokio-based Rust network program involves:

Setting up a runtime and event loop

Initialize the Tokio runtime, which manages the execution of asynchronous tasks.

```
#[tokio::main]

async fn main() {

    // Initialization code

}
```

Creating network sockets

Set up TCP or UDP sockets for network communication.

```
use tokio::net::TcpListener;
```

```
let listener =
TcpListener::bind("127.0.0.1:8080").await.unwrap();
```

Binding sockets to network addresses/ports

Bind the sockets to desired IP addresses and ports to start listening for connections.

```
let addr = "127.0.0.1:8080".to_string();

let listener = TcpListener::bind(&addr).await.unwrap();
```

Registering sockets with event loop

Register the sockets so the event loop can monitor them for incoming data.

```
loop {

    let (socket, _) = listener.accept().await.unwrap();

    tokio::spawn(async move {

        // Handle the connection

    });

}
```

Waiting for incoming data

The event loop waits for events such as data arriving on a socket or a timer expiring.

```
while let Some(Ok(stream)) = listener.next().await {

    tokio::spawn(async move {

        // Process the stream

    });

}
```

Handle each event, such as reading from or writing to a socket.

```
tokio::spawn(async move {

    let mut buf = [0; 1024];

    socket.read(&mut buf).await.unwrap();

    // Process the buffer

});
```

The loop continues to run and keeps handling events until the program exits.

If Statements

Overview

The if statements are used for conditional execution of code based on a boolean expression. This control flow structure allows you to execute different blocks of code depending on whether a condition is true or false.

The syntax of an if statement is as follows:

```
if condition {

    // code to be executed if condition is true

} else {

    // code to be executed if condition is false

}
```

In networking, if statements are particularly useful for handling various conditions that can arise during communication between devices. For example, they can help manage responses from a server, check the status of a connection, or handle errors.

Sample Program: If Statements in a Client-Server Application

Think of a simple client-server application where the client sends a request to the server and the server responds. The client can use if statements to handle different responses from the server and take appropriate action.

Following is an example of a Rust program demonstrating this:

```rust
use std::io::{self, BufRead, Write};

use std::net::TcpStream;



fn main() {
    // Attempt to connect to the server
    match TcpStream::connect("127.0.0.1:8080") {
        Ok(mut stream) => {
            let request = "Hello, server!";
            let mut response = String::new();


            // Send the request to the server
            if
stream.write_all(request.as_bytes()).is_ok() {
                // Read the response from the server
                let mut reader =
io::BufReader::new(&stream);
                if reader.read_line(&mut
response).is_ok() {
                    // Check the response from the server
                    if response.trim() == "OK" {
```

```
                println!("Server responded with
OK");

                } else {

                    println!("Server responded with
an error: {}", response.trim());

                }

            } else {

                println!("Failed to read response
from server");

            }

        } else {

            println!("Failed to send request to
server");

        }

    }

    Err(e) => {

        println!("Failed to connect to server: {}",
e);

    }

    }

}
```

In the above sample program,

- The client attempts to connect to the server using TcpStream::connect("127.0.0.1:8080").

- The match statement is used to handle the result of the connection attempt. If the connection is successful, the stream is used for further communication. If it fails, an error message is printed.

- The client sends a request to the server using stream.write_all(request.as_bytes()). The if statement checks if the request was sent successfully.

- If sending the request fails, an error message is printed.

- If the request is sent successfully, the client reads the server's response using io::BufReader.

- Another if statement checks if reading the response was successful. If it fails, an error message is printed.

- If the response is read successfully, an if statement checks whether the response is "OK".

- If the response is "OK", a success message is printed. Otherwise, an error message containing the server's response is printed.

In addition, if statements also allow you to handle various other scenarios and conditions, and that too effectively. For instance, you can:

1. Check if the responses from the server are as expected and handle different types of responses appropriately.

2. Manage errors gracefully by checking if operations succeed or fail and taking appropriate actions.

3. Perform different actions based on the status of connections, data integrity, or other conditions.

If statements are fundamental to controlling the flow of a Rust program, especially in networking applications where handling different conditions and responses is critical.

Loop Statements

Loop statements are used to execute a block of code repeatedly until a certain condition is met or the loop is explicitly broken. In networking applications, loops are particularly useful for continuously listening for incoming connections or data, ensuring that the program remains responsive and handles multiple requests effectively.

Sample Program: Using Loop for Networking

Given below is an example of how loop statements can be used in a Rust networking program:

```
use std::net::TcpListener;
```

```rust
fn main() {

    let listener =
TcpListener::bind("127.0.0.1:8080").unwrap();

    println!("Listening on port 8080...");


    loop {

        match listener.accept() {

            Ok((socket, addr)) => {

                println!("New connection: {}", addr);


                // Handle incoming data on a separate
thread

                std::thread::spawn(move || {

                    handle_connection(socket);

                });

            }

            Err(e) => {

                eprintln!("Error accepting connection:
{}", e);

            }

        }
```

```
    }

}


fn handle_connection(mut socket: std::net::TcpStream) {

    // Read data from the socket and handle it

    // ...

}
```

In the above code snippet,

- The TcpListener::bind function binds the listener to the specified address (127.0.0.1:8080) and starts listening for incoming connections. If binding fails, the program will panic (unwrap), but in a real-world scenario, you would handle this error more gracefully as below:

```
let listener =
TcpListener::bind("127.0.0.1:8080").unwrap();

println!("Listening on port 8080...");
```

- The loop statement starts an infinite loop that will run until the program is terminated or explicitly broken out of.

```
loop {

    // Code to handle incoming connections

}
```

- Within the loop, the listener.accept() method waits for a new connection. The match statement handles the result of this method. If a connection is successfully accepted, a message is printed, and the handle_connection function is called on a separate thread using std::thread::spawn.

```rust
match listener.accept() {

  Ok((socket, addr)) => {

        println!("New connection: {}", addr);


        std::thread::spawn(move || {

            handle_connection(socket);

        });

  }

  Err(e) => {

        eprintln!("Error accepting connection: {}", e);

  }

}
```

- The handle_connection function is responsible for reading data from the socket and handling it. This function is run on a separate thread for each incoming connection, allowing the program to handle multiple connections simultaneously.

```rust
fn handle_connection(mut socket: std::net::TcpStream) {

    // Read data from the socket and handle it

    // ...

}
```

Loop Benefits in Networking

- Loop statements allow the server to continuously listen for and accept incoming connections, ensuring that it remains available to clients at all times.

- By spawning a new thread for each connection, the server can handle multiple connections simultaneously, improving responsiveness and scalability.

- The match statement within the loop provides a structured way to handle errors that may occur when accepting connections, ensuring that the server can continue running even if an error occurs.

- The use of functions like handle_connection allows for modular code design, making the program easier to read, maintain, and extend.

Enhancements and Best Practices

Graceful Error Handling

Instead of using unwrap, handle errors gracefully to ensure the server can recover from failures without crashing.

```
let listener =
TcpListener::bind("127.0.0.1:8080").expect("Could not
bind to address");
```

Configurable Parameters

Use configuration files or environment variables to set parameters like the IP address and port number, making the server more flexible and easier to deploy in different environments.

```
let address =
std::env::var("SERVER_ADDRESS").unwrap_or("127.0.0.1:8080
".to_string());

let listener = TcpListener::bind(&address).expect("Could
not bind to address");
```

Logging

Use a logging library to manage output, providing more control over logging levels and output formats.

```
use log::{info, error};

use std::net::TcpListener;
```

```rust
fn main() {

    env_logger::init();

    let listener =
TcpListener::bind("127.0.0.1:8080").expect("Could not
bind to address");

    info!("Listening on port 8080...");


    loop {

        match listener.accept() {

            Ok((socket, addr)) => {

                info!("New connection: {}", addr);


                std::thread::spawn(move || {

                    handle_connection(socket);

                });

            }

            Err(e) => {

                error!("Error accepting connection: {}",
e);

            }

        }
```

```
        }

}
```

A combination of loop statements and concurrency features, such as thread spawning, makes it possible to build large and responsive network servers. These networking programs are even more robust and easier to maintain when they use proper error handling and have modular code design.

While Statements

While statements are used to create loops that execute a block of code repeatedly as long as a specified condition remains true. This is particularly useful where operations need to be performed continuously until certain conditions are met. For instance, receiving data from a socket until a complete message is received can be efficiently handled using a while loop.

Sample Program: Using While Statements

Following is an example demonstrating how a while loop can be used to receive data from a socket:

```
use std::io::prelude::*;

use std::net::TcpStream;



fn main() -> std::io::Result<()> {

    // Establish a connection to the server

    let mut stream =
TcpStream::connect("127.0.0.1:8080")?;


    // Buffer for incoming data

    let mut buf = [0; 1024];

    // String to accumulate the complete message
```

```
    let mut message = String::new();


    // Loop until the message contains at least two
newline characters
    while message.chars().filter(|&c| c == '\n').count()
< 2 {

        // Read data from the stream into the buffer

        let bytes_read = stream.read(&mut buf)?;

        // Append the buffer contents to the message
string

message.push_str(&String::from_utf8_lossy(&buf[..bytes_re
ad]));

    }


    // Print out the received message

    println!("Received message: {}", message);


    Ok(())

}
```

In the above sample program,

- The TcpStream::connect function establishes a connection to a server at the specified
  address (127.0.0.1:8080). If the connection fails, it returns an error.

```rust
let mut stream = TcpStream::connect("127.0.0.1:8080")?;
```

- A buffer (buf) of 1024 bytes is created to store incoming data.
- A string (message) is initialized to accumulate the complete message from the server.

```rust
let mut buf = [0; 1024];

let mut message = String::new();
```

- The while loop condition checks if the message contains fewer than two newline characters (\n). The loop continues running until this condition is false.

```rust
while message.chars().filter(|&c| c == '\n').count() < 2
{
    // Read data from the stream into the buffer

    let bytes_read = stream.read(&mut buf)?;

    // Append the buffer contents to the message string


message.push_str(&String::from_utf8_lossy(&buf[..bytes_re
ad]));

}
```

- Inside the loop, data is read from the stream into the buffer using stream.read(&mut buf). The read data (converted from raw bytes to a UTF-8 string) is appended to the message string using push_str.
- Once the while loop exits (when the message contains at least two newline characters), the complete message is printed.

```rust
println!("Received message: {}", message);
```

Sample Program: Handling Multiple Messages

Given below is an improvised example where the program continues to receive and process multiple messages:

```rust
use std::io::prelude::*;

use std::net::TcpStream;


fn main() -> std::io::Result<()> {

    let mut stream =
TcpStream::connect("127.0.0.1:8080")?;

    let mut buf = [0; 1024];

    let mut message = String::new();


    // Loop to handle multiple messages

    loop {

        while !message.ends_with("\n\n") {

            let bytes_read = stream.read(&mut buf)?;

            if bytes_read == 0 {

                println!("Connection closed by server");

                return Ok(());

            }

message.push_str(&String::from_utf8_lossy(&buf[..bytes_read]));

        }
```

```
        // Process the complete message

        println!("Received message: {}",
message.trim_end());


        // Clear the message for the next iteration

        message.clear();

    }

}
```

In the above modified sample program,

- The loop continues to handle multiple messages until the connection is closed.
- And, the message string is cleared after processing each complete message, ready to accumulate the next message.

For Statements

The for loop is used to iterate over a range, a collection, or any object that implements the Iterator trait. This loop plays its charm for tasks such as processing a list of network requests, iterating over a range of values for constructing network packets, or reading data from a network stream.

Basic Syntax

The basic syntax for a for loop is as follows:

```
for item in collection {

    // loop body

}
```

In this syntax:

- item represents the current element being iterated over.
- collection represents the range or collection of elements to iterate over.
- The loop body contains the code to be executed for each iteration.

Sample Program: Iterating Over Network Addresses

Given below is an example of how a for loop can be used to iterate over a collection of network addresses and attempt to establish a connection to each of them:

```rust
use std::net::TcpStream;

use std::io::{Read, Write};



fn main() {

    let addresses = ["127.0.0.1:8080",
"gitforgits.com:80", "192.168.1.1:22"];



    for addr in addresses.iter() {

        match TcpStream::connect(addr) {

            Ok(mut stream) => {

                println!("Connected to {}", addr);



                // Send data to the server

                let data = b"Hello, server!";

                stream.write_all(data).unwrap();



                // Read response from the server
```

```
                let mut buf = [0; 128];

                let n = stream.read(&mut buf).unwrap();

                println!("Server response: {}",
String::from_utf8_lossy(&buf[..n]));

            }

            Err(e) => {

                println!("Failed to connect to {}: {}",
addr, e);

            }

        }

    }

}
```

Now, in the above code snippet,

- A collection of network addresses is defined as an array as below:

```
let addresses = ["127.0.0.1:8080", "gitforgits.com:80",
"192.168.1.1:22"];
```

- The for loop iterates over each address in the addresses array. The .iter() method is used to obtain an iterator over the array.

```
for addr in addresses.iter() {

    // Attempt to connect to each address

}
```

- For each address, a TCP connection is attempted using TcpStream::connect(addr). The match statement handles the result of the connection attempt. If the connection is successful, a message is printed, data is sent to the server, and the server's response is read and printed. If the connection fails, an error message is printed.

```
match TcpStream::connect(addr) {

    Ok(mut stream) => {

        println!("Connected to {}", addr);


        // Send data to the server

        let data = b"Hello, server!";

        stream.write_all(data).unwrap();


        // Read response from the server

        let mut buf = [0; 128];

        let n = stream.read(&mut buf).unwrap();

        println!("Server response: {}",
String::from_utf8_lossy(&buf[..n]));

    }

    Err(e) => {

        println!("Failed to connect to {}: {}", addr, e);

    }

}
```

For Loops Applications

- A for loop can be used to iterate over a list of incoming network requests, processing each one in turn.

- When constructing network packets, a for loop can iterate over a range of values to fill packet fields or headers.
- In scenarios where data is streamed over a network connection, a for loop can be used to read chunks of data from the stream and process them sequentially.

Sample Program: Handling a List of Network Requests

Given below is a more complex example where a for loop is used to process a list of network requests from multiple clients:

```rust
use std::net::{TcpListener, TcpStream};

use std::io::{Read, Write};

use std::thread;


fn handle_client(mut stream: TcpStream) {

    let mut buf = [0; 512];

    while let Ok(bytes_read) = stream.read(&mut buf) {

        if bytes_read == 0 {

            return;

        }

        // Echo the data back to the client

        stream.write_all(&buf[..bytes_read]).unwrap();

    }

}


fn main() -> std::io::Result<()> {
```

```
let listener = TcpListener::bind("127.0.0.1:8080")?;

println!("Server listening on port 8080");


for stream in listener.incoming() {

    match stream {

        Ok(stream) => {

            thread::spawn(|| {

                handle_client(stream);

            });

        }

        Err(e) => {

            eprintln!("Failed to accept connection:
{}", e);

        }

    }

}

Ok(())

}
```

In the above given example,

- A TcpListener is set up to accept incoming connections on port 8080.
- A for loop iterates over the incoming connections.
- Each connection is handled in a separate thread using thread::spawn, allowing the server to handle multiple clients simultaneously.

Tasks like processing network requests, creating network packets, and reading data streams are well-suited to the for loop because of its versatility and power, which enable efficient repetition over ranges and collections.

Pattern Matching

Pattern matching enables us to match different patterns against a value and execute corresponding code. In networking, pattern matching can be used to handle various types of network events, such as different types of messages or requests. This capability is provided by the match expression.

Basic Syntax

The match expression takes an expression to match against and a series of arms. Each arm contains a pattern and the corresponding code to execute if the pattern matches the value.

```
match expression {

    pattern1 => code_to_execute_if_pattern1_matches,

    pattern2 => code_to_execute_if_pattern2_matches,

    _ => code_to_execute_if_no_patterns_match, // _ is a
catch-all pattern

}
```

Sample Program: Implement Pattern Matching

Given below is an example of using pattern matching in a simple Rust networking application:

```
use std::net::{TcpListener, TcpStream};

use std::io::{Read, Write};


fn handle_client(mut stream: TcpStream) {

    let mut buf = [0; 512];
```

```rust
    match stream.read(&mut buf) {

        Ok(n) => {

            let request =
String::from_utf8_lossy(&buf[..n]);

            println!("Received request: {}", request);

            match request.as_ref() {

                "GET /hello HTTP/1.1\r\n" => {

                    let response = "HTTP/1.1 200
OK\r\n\r\nHello, world!";

stream.write_all(response.as_bytes()).unwrap();

                },

                _ => {

                    let response = "HTTP/1.1 404 NOT
FOUND\r\n\r\n";

stream.write_all(response.as_bytes()).unwrap();

                }

            }

        },

        Err(e) => {

            println!("Error reading from socket: {}", e);

        }
```

```rust
        }
    }


fn main() {
    let listener =
TcpListener::bind("127.0.0.1:8080").unwrap();

    for stream in listener.incoming() {

        match stream {

            Ok(stream) => {

                println!("New client connected: {}",
stream.peer_addr().unwrap());

                std::thread::spawn(|| {

                    handle_client(stream);

                });

            }

            Err(e) => {

                println!("Error accepting client: {}",
e);

            }

        }

    }

}
```

In the above implementation program,

- A TcpListener is created to listen on the address 127.0.0.1:8080. The listener accepts incoming connections.

```
let listener =
TcpListener::bind("127.0.0.1:8080").unwrap();
```

- The for loop iterates over incoming connections. Each connection is handled using a match expression. If a connection is successfully accepted (Ok(stream)), a new thread is spawned to handle the client connection. If there is an error (Err(e)), an error message is printed.

```
for stream in listener.incoming() {

    match stream {

        Ok(stream) => {

            println!("New client connected: {}",
stream.peer_addr().unwrap());

            std::thread::spawn(|| {

                handle_client(stream);

            });

        }

        Err(e) => {

            println!("Error accepting client: {}", e);

        }

    }

}
```

- The handle_client function reads data from the client using stream.read. The result of the read operation is matched using a match expression. If reading data is successful (Ok(n)), the bytes read are converted to a string (request), and another match expression is used to match the request string against predefined patterns. If the request is "GET /hello HTTP/1.1\r\n", a response with "Hello, world!" is sent back to the client.

- For any other request, a "404 NOT FOUND" response is sent. If there is an error reading from the socket (Err(e)), an error message is printed.

```rust
fn handle_client(mut stream: TcpStream) {

    let mut buf = [0; 512];

    match stream.read(&mut buf) {

        Ok(n) => {

            let request =
String::from_utf8_lossy(&buf[..n]);

            println!("Received request: {}", request);

            match request.as_ref() {

                "GET /hello HTTP/1.1\r\n" => {

                    let response = "HTTP/1.1 200
OK\r\n\r\nHello, world!";

stream.write_all(response.as_bytes()).unwrap();

                },

                _ => {

                    let response = "HTTP/1.1 404 NOT
FOUND\r\n\r\n";

stream.write_all(response.as_bytes()).unwrap();
```

```rust
                    }
                }
            },
        Err(e) => {
            println!("Error reading from socket: {}", e);
        }
    }
}
```

In a messaging application, you can use pattern matching to handle different types of messages (e.g., text, image, video) based on the message type. In a protocol implementation, pattern matching can be used to process different commands and responses based on the protocol specification. Pattern matching can also be used to handle different error conditions in network operations, such as connection timeouts, data corruption, and protocol violations. Pattern matching is a powerful feature that enhances the flexibility and readability of networking code.

Summary

In this chapter, we have covered some of the fundamental concepts of Rust programming language, particularly variables, constants, functions, control flow, if, while, loop, for statements, and pattern matching. Variables are mutable by default in Rust, and can be defined using the let keyword followed by the variable name and the value. Constants, on the other hand, are immutable and can be defined using the const keyword. Functions are defined using the fn keyword, and can have arguments and a return type.

Control flow statements like if are used to perform conditional operations, while loops are used to repeat operations until a certain condition is met, and for loops are used to perform a certain operation for a specified number of times. Pattern matching allows us to match the structure of data with a corresponding pattern and execute certain code accordingly. In the next chapter, we will introduce Rust's ownership and borrowing system, which is used to manage memory allocation and deallocation and how these concepts can be applied in the context of network programming.

CHAPTER 4: CORE RUST FOR NETWORKS

Mutability

Overview

By default, all variables are immutable, meaning that once you assign a value to a variable, you cannot change it. However, you can make a variable mutable by using the mut keyword before the variable name. This feature is needed to update the state of a connection or a data structure.

Following are the benefits of mutability in networking:

1. Mutability allows dynamic updates to the state of network connections and data structures, enabling more flexible and responsive network applications.

2. By allowing in-place modifications of data structures, mutability avoids the overhead of creating new instances, leading to more efficient memory and performance management.

3. In multi-threaded network applications, mutable variables can be safely shared and updated across threads using synchronization primitives, such as Mutex and RwLock.

Importance of Mutability

Mutability plays a crucial role in various scenarios:

- Updating the State of a Connection

Network connections are often long-lived and can change over time. Mutability allows you to update the state of a connection, such as changing its timeout value, closing the connection, or updating its read buffer.

- Modifying Data Structures

Network programming frequently involves modifying data structures, such as a message buffer, to reflect changes in the network. Mutability allows you to modify these data structures without creating a new instance of the structure.

- Sharing Data Between Threads

Network programming often involves multiple threads that communicate through shared data structures. Mutability is essential for thread synchronization and ensuring that data is accessed and modified safely.

Sample Program: Mutability in a Simple TCP Server

Suppose you are building a simple server that listens for connections on a TCP port and prints the received messages to the console. Given below is how you can use mutability to update the state of the connection and the message buffer:

```rust
use std::io::prelude::*;
use std::net::TcpListener;
use std::net::TcpStream;


fn main() -> std::io::Result<()> {
    // Bind the TCP listener to the specified address and port
    let listener = TcpListener::bind("127.0.0.1:8080")?;


    // Iterate over incoming connections
    for stream in listener.incoming() {
        // Create a mutable stream variable
        let mut stream = stream?;


        // Create a mutable buffer to store incoming data
        let mut buffer = [0; 1024];


        // Loop to read data from the stream
        loop {
            // Read data into the buffer
            let bytes_read = stream.read(&mut buffer)?;
```

```rust
            // Break the loop if no data is read
            if bytes_read == 0 {
                break;
            }


            // Convert the bytes to a string and print
the message
            let message =
String::from_utf8_lossy(&buffer[0..bytes_read]);
            println!("Received message: {}", message);
        }
    }


    Ok(())
}
```

In the above sample program,

- The TcpListener::bind function binds the listener to the specified address (127.0.0.1:8080) and starts listening for incoming connections.

```rust
let listener = TcpListener::bind("127.0.0.1:8080")?;
```

- The for loop iterates over incoming connections. For each connection, we create a mutable stream variable.

```rust
for stream in listener.incoming() {

    let mut stream = stream?;
```

```
}
```

- A mutable buffer (buffer) of 1024 bytes is created to store incoming data.

```
let mut buffer = [0; 1024]
```

- A loop statement reads data from the stream into the buffer. The mut keyword allows us to modify the buffer and stream variables. The stream.read(&mut buffer) method reads data into the buffer, and the number of bytes read is stored in bytes_read.

```
loop {

    let bytes_read = stream.read(&mut buffer)?;

    if bytes_read == 0 {

        break;

    }

    let message =
String::from_utf8_lossy(&buffer[0..bytes_read]);

    println!("Received message: {}", message);

}
```

Sample Program: Updating a Shared Data Structure

Following is an example of using mutability with shared data structures in a multi-threaded context:

```
use std::sync::{Arc, Mutex};

use std::thread;

use std::net::TcpListener;

use std::io::prelude::*;
```

```
fn main() -> std::io::Result<()> {

    let listener = TcpListener::bind("127.0.0.1:8080")?;

    let message_count = Arc::new(Mutex::new(0));


    for stream in listener.incoming() {

        let stream = stream?;

        let message_count = Arc::clone(&message_count);


        thread::spawn(move || {

            let mut stream = stream;

            let mut buffer = [0; 1024];


            loop {

                let bytes_read = stream.read(&mut
buffer).unwrap();

                if bytes_read == 0 {

                    break;

                }


                let message =
String::from_utf8_lossy(&buffer[0..bytes_read]);
```

```
            println!("Received message: {}",
message);


            let mut count =
message_count.lock().unwrap();

            *count += 1;

            println!("Message count: {}", count);

        }

    });

  }

  Ok(())

}
```

In the above example,

- An Arc<Mutex<>> is used to share the message_count across multiple threads safely.
- Each thread updates the message_count when it receives a message, demonstrating safe concurrent modifications.

Rust accomplishes dynamic state management, efficient data handling, and secure concurrency in network applications by permitting variables to be modified. Using the synchronization primitives and the mut keyword with care, Rust developers may create networked systems that are both robust and fast.

Ownership

Overview

Ownership is a fundamental concept that ensures memory safety without the need for a garbage collector. Each value in Rust has an owner, which is responsible for managing its lifetime and freeing the associated memory when the value is no longer needed. This mechanism plays an essential role where efficient and safe management of resources like sockets and buffers is critical.

Ownership is implemented through a set of rules that govern how values can be moved, borrowed, or lent. The primary rule is that a value can have only one owner at a time, and this owner has the exclusive right to modify or destroy the value. This rule prevents multiple threads from accessing the same data simultaneously, which can cause race conditions and synchronization issues.

Following are the benefits of ownership to networking applications:

1. Ownership ensures that resources like sockets and buffers are properly managed and cleaned up when no longer needed, preventing resource leaks.

2. Rust's ownership model helps prevent data races and ensures safe access to shared data in concurrent network applications. Shared data can be accessed safely using synchronization primitives like Mutex and RwLock.

3. By allowing in-place modifications and avoiding unnecessary copies, Rust's ownership model enables efficient handling of large amounts of data in network applications.

Sample Program: Implementing Ownership

To understand ownership in the context of network programming, take an example of a simple server that listens for incoming connections and echoes back any data it receives from clients.

Following is the code for the server:

```
use std::io::prelude::*;

use std::net::{TcpListener, TcpStream};


fn main() -> std::io::Result<()> {

    // Bind the listener to the address and port

    let listener = TcpListener::bind("127.0.0.1:8080")?;

    println!("Listening on port 8080...");


    // Iterate over incoming connections

    for stream in listener.incoming() {
```

```rust
        // Take ownership of the TcpStream object
        let mut stream = stream?;
        println!("New client connected: {:?}",
stream.peer_addr()?);


        // Buffer to store incoming data
        let mut buf = [0; 1024];


        // Loop to read data from the stream
        loop {
            // Read data into the buffer
            let bytes_read = stream.read(&mut buf)?;
            if bytes_read == 0 {
                println!("Client disconnected");
                break;
            }


            // Echo the received data back to the client
            stream.write_all(&buf[..bytes_read])?;
        }
    }
```

```
    Ok(())
}
```

In the above sample program,

- The TcpListener::bind function binds the listener to the specified address (127.0.0.1:8080) and starts listening for incoming connections.

```
let listener = TcpListener::bind("127.0.0.1:8080")?;

println!("Listening on port 8080...");
```

- The for loop iterates over incoming connections. The listener.incoming() method returns an iterator that produces a sequence of TcpStream objects representing these connections. The for loop takes ownership of each TcpStream object in turn and binds it to the variable stream.

```
for stream in listener.incoming() {

    let mut stream = stream?;

    println!("New client connected: {:?}",
stream.peer_addr()?);

}
```

- Within the loop, a buffer (buf) is created to store incoming data. This buffer is stack-allocated and reused for each incoming connection, making it more efficient than dynamically allocating a new buffer for each connection. The loop reads data from the stream into the buffer and then writes the data back to the client, effectively echoing the received data.

```
let mut buf = [0; 1024];


loop {

    let bytes_read = stream.read(&mut buf)?;
```

```
    if bytes_read == 0 {

        println!("Client disconnected");

        break;

    }


    stream.write_all(&buf[..bytes_read])?;

}
```

Each TcpStream object is owned by the for loop during each iteration. This ownership ensures that only one part of the code has access to the stream at any given time, preventing race conditions. The buffer (buf) is reused for each connection. Since it is stack-allocated, it does not require dynamic memory management, reducing the risk of memory leaks. The stream object is mutable, allowing the loop to read from and write to the stream. This mutability is necessary for updating the state of the connection. When the loop exits, the stream object is dropped, and its associated resources are freed automatically by Rust's ownership system. This automatic cleanup ensures efficient resource management.

With ownership, there is no need for a garbage collector, since memory is safe and resources are managed efficiently. Having clear ownership makes managing resources like buffers, connections, and more efficient and secure.

Borrowing

Overview

Borrowing is a mechanism that allows a program to pass a reference to a value or resource to a function or code block without transferring ownership of that value or resource. This means that the function or code block can access and modify the value or resource but does not take ownership of it. Borrowing is essential in many scenarios, including network programming, to prevent resource leaks and improve program efficiency.

When writing network programs, it is often necessary to pass references to data buffers, network sockets, or other resources to functions or code blocks. Borrowing allows these references to be passed without transferring ownership, thus maintaining control over resource management and avoiding duplication of resources.

Sample Program: Using Borrowing

We will take a simple Rust program that creates a TCP listener and accepts incoming connections. When a new connection is accepted, the program creates a new thread to handle the connection. Borrowing can be used to pass a reference to the new connection socket to the thread without transferring ownership of the socket.

```rust
use std::net::{TcpListener, TcpStream};

use std::thread;



fn handle_connection(stream: &mut TcpStream) {

    // handle the connection

    let mut buffer = [0; 512];

    loop {

        match stream.read(&mut buffer) {

            Ok(0) => {

                println!("Connection closed");

                break;

            }

            Ok(n) => {

                println!("Received data: {}",
String::from_utf8_lossy(&buffer[..n]));

                if
stream.write_all(&buffer[..n]).is_err() {

                    println!("Failed to send data");

                    break;
```

```rust
                }
            }
            Err(e) => {
                println!("Error reading from stream: {}",
e);
                break;
            }
        }
    }
}


fn main() {
    let listener =
TcpListener::bind("127.0.0.1:8080").unwrap();


    for stream in listener.incoming() {
        match stream {
            Ok(stream) => {
                // pass a reference to the socket to the
new thread
                thread::spawn(move || {
                    handle_connection(&mut
stream.try_clone().unwrap());
```

```
        });

    }

    Err(e) => {

        println!("Error: {}", e);

    }

    }

    }

}
```

In the above sample program,

- The handle_connection function takes a mutable reference to a TcpStream object. This allows the function to read from and write to the stream without taking ownership of it.

```
fn handle_connection(stream: &mut TcpStream) {

    let mut buffer = [0; 512];

    loop {

        match stream.read(&mut buffer) {

            Ok(0) => {

                println!("Connection closed");

                break;

            }

            Ok(n) => {

                println!("Received data: {}",
String::from_utf8_lossy(&buffer[..n]));
```

```rust
                if
stream.write_all(&buffer[..n]).is_err() {

                    println!("Failed to send data");

                    break;

                }

            }

            Err(e) => {

                println!("Error reading from stream: {}",
e);

                break;

            }

        }

    }
}
```

- The TcpListener::bind function binds the listener to the specified address (127.0.0.1:8080) and starts listening for incoming connections.

```rust
let listener =
TcpListener::bind("127.0.0.1:8080").unwrap();
```

- The for loop iterates over incoming connections. For each connection, it creates a new thread and passes a mutable reference to the TcpStream object using the &mut syntax. The try_clone method is used to create a new, independent reference to the socket, which can be safely passed to the new thread.

```rust
for stream in listener.incoming() {

    match stream {
```

```
        Ok(stream) => {

            thread::spawn(move || {

                handle_connection(&mut
stream.try_clone().unwrap());

            });

        }

        Err(e) => {

            println!("Error: {}", e);

        }

    }

}
```

Borrowing for Data Buffers

Another use case for borrowing is when working with data buffers. For example, when receiving data from a network socket, it is often necessary to read the data into a buffer and process it. By using borrowing, it is possible to pass a reference to the buffer to the code that processes the data, without transferring ownership of the buffer.

```
use std::io::Read;

use std::net::TcpStream;


fn handle_data(buffer: &mut [u8]) {

    // process the data

    println!("Processing data: {}",
String::from_utf8_lossy(buffer));
```

```rust
}


fn main() {

    let mut stream =
TcpStream::connect("127.0.0.1:8080").unwrap();

    let mut buffer = [0; 1024];


    loop {

        match stream.read(&mut buffer) {

            Ok(n) => {

                if n == 0 {

                    println!("Connection closed");

                    break;

                }

                // pass a reference to the buffer to the
data processing function

                handle_data(&mut buffer[..n]);

            }

            Err(e) => {

                println!("Error: {}", e);

                break;

            }
```

```
        }

    }

}
```

In the above,

- The handle_data function takes a mutable reference to a slice of bytes, representing the data received from the network socket. This allows the function to process the data without taking ownership of the buffer.

```
fn handle_data(buffer: &mut [u8]) {

    println!("Processing data: {}",
String::from_utf8_lossy(buffer));

}
```

- The main loop reads data from the stream into a buffer and then passes a reference to the buffer slice to the handle_data function using the &mut syntax.

```
let mut buffer = [0; 1024];


loop {

    match stream.read(&mut buffer) {

        Ok(n) => {

            if n == 0 {

                println!("Connection closed");

                break;

            }

            handle_data(&mut buffer[..n]);
```

```
        }

        Err(e) => {

            println!("Error: {}", e);

            break;

        }

    }

}
```

It is now obvious that borrowing allows functions or blocks of code to receive references to resources like data buffers and network sockets, which guarantees that these resources are maintained correctly and effectively.

Structs

Overview

A struct is a custom data type that allows you to group related pieces of data together under a single name. Structs are commonly used to represent various components of a networked system, such as a packet header, a socket address, or a network interface configuration.

A struct can be defined using the struct keyword, followed by the name of the struct and a list of its fields. Given below is an example of a simple struct representing a TCP socket address:

```
use std::net::{IpAddr, Ipv4Addr};


struct TcpSocketAddr {

    ip: IpAddr,

    port: u16,

}
```

In the above code snippet, TcpSocketAddr is the name of the struct, ip is a field that holds an IpAddr value, and port is a field that holds a u16 (16-bit unsigned integer) value.

Creating Instances of a Struct

You can create a new instance of a struct using its constructor function, which is the name of the struct followed by a set of curly braces containing the values of its fields:

```
let addr = TcpSocketAddr {

    ip: IpAddr::V4(Ipv4Addr::new(127, 0, 0, 1)),

    port: 8080,

};
```

In the above code snippet, addr is a new instance of the TcpSocketAddr struct, with its ip field set to the IPv4 loopback address (127.0.0.1) and its port field set to 8080.

Methods on Structs

Structs can also have methods, which are functions that operate on instances of the struct. Given below is an example of a method that returns a string representation of a TcpSocketAddr:

```
impl TcpSocketAddr {

    fn to_string(&self) -> String {

        format!("{}:{}", self.ip, self.port)

    }

}
```

In the above code snippet, the impl keyword introduces an implementation block for the TcpSocketAddr struct, and the to_string method takes a reference to self (the instance of the struct) and returns a string that combines the string representations of its ip and port fields.

You can call this method on a TcpSocketAddr instance like this:

```
let addr = TcpSocketAddr {
```

```
    ip: IpAddr::V4(Ipv4Addr::new(127, 0, 0, 1)),

    port: 8080,

};

println!("Address: {}", addr.to_string());
```

In the above code snippet, the to_string method is called on the addr instance, which prints "127.0.0.1:8080" to the console.

Sample Program: Struct for Packet Header

Let us take an example where you might use a struct to represent a packet header, which could contain fields such as the packet length, protocol type, and checksum value. By grouping these fields together in a struct, you can easily pass the entire header as a single value to various functions that operate on it.

Following is an example struct representing a packet header:

```
struct PacketHeader {

    length: u16,

    protocol: u8,

    checksum: u16,

}
```

You can create an instance of PacketHeader and use it in functions as follows:

```
fn process_packet(header: &PacketHeader) {

    println!(

        "Processing packet: length = {}, protocol = {},
checksum = {}",

        header.length, header.protocol, header.checksum
```

```
    );

}


fn main() {

    let header = PacketHeader {

        length: 512,

        protocol: 1,

        checksum: 0xffff,

    };


    process_packet(&header);

}
```

In the above code snippet, the process_packet function takes a reference to a PacketHeader instance and prints its fields. The main function creates a PacketHeader instance and passes it to process_packet.

Sample Program: Struct for Network Interface Configuration

Another practical use case for structs is representing network interface configurations. For example, you can define a struct to represent the configuration of a network interface:

```
use std::net::Ipv4Addr;


struct NetworkConfig {

    ip: Ipv4Addr,
```

```rust
    subnet_mask: Ipv4Addr,

    gateway: Ipv4Addr,

}


impl NetworkConfig {

    fn display_config(&self) {

        println!("IP Address: {}", self.ip);

        println!("Subnet Mask: {}", self.subnet_mask);

        println!("Gateway: {}", self.gateway);

    }

}


fn main() {

    let config = NetworkConfig {

        ip: Ipv4Addr::new(192, 168, 1, 10),

        subnet_mask: Ipv4Addr::new(255, 255, 255, 0),

        gateway: Ipv4Addr::new(192, 168, 1, 1),

    };


    config.display_config();

}
```

In the above code snippet, the NetworkConfig struct contains fields for the IP address, subnet mask, and gateway. The display_config method prints these values to the console. The main function creates an instance of NetworkConfig and calls display_config. Whether representing a TCP socket address, a packet header, or a network configuration, structs are an essential tool in the Rust programmer's toolkit.

Enums & Pattern Matching

Overview

Enums allow developers to define a type by enumerating its possible variants. This feature makes the code more expressive, safer, and easier to reason about. Enums are particularly useful to represent different types of messages exchanged between clients and servers.

An enum is defined using the enum keyword, followed by the name of the enum and a list of variants. Each variant can optionally have associated data.

```
enum Message {

    Join,

    Leave,

    Text(String),

    Ping,

    Pong,

}
```

In the above given example,

- Message is the name of the enum.

- The variants Join and Leave do not have any associated data.

- The variant Text has an associated String value, which can contain the text of the message.

- The variants Ping and Pong do not have any associated data.

Pattern Matching

One of the key features of enums is pattern matching, which allows developers to easily extract and use the data associated with an enum variant.

```rust
fn process_message(message: Message) {

    match message {

        Message::Join => println!("A user has joined the chat"),

        Message::Leave => println!("A user has left the chat"),

        Message::Text(text) => println!("Received message: {}", text),

        Message::Ping => println!("Received ping"),

        Message::Pong => println!("Received pong"),

    }

}
```

In the above code snippet, the process_message function takes a Message as input and uses a match statement to handle each variant.

Using Enums in Message Protocol

Enums are widely used to represent different types of messages that can be exchanged between clients and servers. Given below is an example of a simple messaging protocol using an enum:

```rust
enum ProtocolMessage {

    Login { username: String, password: String },

    Logout,

    Chat { from: String, message: String },

    Error { code: u16, message: String },
```

```
}
```

In the above given example,

- ProtocolMessage enum has four variants.
- Login variant has associated String values for username and password.
- Chat variant has associated String values for the sender (from) and the message (message).
- Error variant has an error code (code) and an error message (message).

Sample Program: Using ProtocolMessage Enum

Following is an example of how to use the ProtocolMessage enum in a simple server application:

```
use std::net::{TcpListener, TcpStream};

use std::io::{Read, Write};

use std::thread;


fn handle_client(mut stream: TcpStream) {

    let mut buffer = [0; 512];

    loop {

        let bytes_read = stream.read(&mut
buffer).unwrap();

        if bytes_read == 0 {

            println!("Client disconnected");

            break;

        }
```

```rust
        let received_data =
String::from_utf8_lossy(&buffer[..bytes_read]);

        let protocol_message: ProtocolMessage =
serde_json::from_str(&received_data).unwrap();


        match protocol_message {

            ProtocolMessage::Login { username, password }
=> {

                println!("User {} logged in with password
{}", username, password);

            },

            ProtocolMessage::Logout => {

                println!("User logged out");

            },

            ProtocolMessage::Chat { from, message } => {

                println!("{} says: {}", from, message);

            },

            ProtocolMessage::Error { code, message } => {

                println!("Error {}: {}", code, message);

            },

        }

    }

}
```

```rust
fn main() {

    let listener =
TcpListener::bind("127.0.0.1:8080").unwrap();

    println!("Server listening on port 8080");


    for stream in listener.incoming() {

        match stream {

            Ok(stream) => {

                thread::spawn(move || {

                    handle_client(stream);

                });

            }

            Err(e) => {

                println!("Failed to accept connection:
{}", e);

            }

        }

    }

}
```

In the above given example,

- The handle_client function reads data from the client and deserializes it into a ProtocolMessage.

- Pattern matching is used to handle each variant of ProtocolMessage.

Data Enumeration

Rust enums can also have associated data using structs, known as data enumerations.

```
enum Message {

    Quit,

    Move { x: i32, y: i32 },

    Write(String),

    ChangeColor(i32, i32, i32),

}
```

In the above given example,

- Quit is a simple variant without data.
- Move variant has two fields, x and y, which are both i32.
- Write variant has a String field.
- ChangeColor variant has three i32 fields.

Sample Program: Client Messages in Chat App

Following is an example of using enums to represent different client messages in a chat application:

```
enum ClientMessage {

    Join(String),

    Leave,

    Chat(String),

    Whisper { to: String, msg: String },

}
```

```rust
fn handle_client_message(client_message: ClientMessage) {

    match client_message {

        ClientMessage::Join(name) => {

            println!("{} joined the chat", name);

        },

        ClientMessage::Leave => {

            println!("A user left the chat");

        },

        ClientMessage::Chat(msg) => {

            println!("Chat message: {}", msg);

        },

        ClientMessage::Whisper { to, msg } => {

            println!("Whisper to {}: {}", to, msg);

        },

    }

}
```

In the above example, the ClientMessage enum variations stand for the various client-side message types. To properly handle each message type, the handle_client_message function use pattern matching. The use of enums and pattern matching allows Rust developers to create networked programs that are both strong and easy to maintain.

Traits

Overview

Traits are a powerful feature that allows for polymorphism and code reuse in an efficient and type-safe manner. Traits enable you to define shared behavior across different types, where different protocols like TCP, UDP, and HTTP can share common methods such as connecting, sending, and receiving data.

Now, to define a trait, you use the trait keyword followed by the name of the trait and a set of method signatures. Given below is an example:

```
trait NetworkProtocol {

    fn connect(&mut self, address: &str) -> Result<(),
String>;

    fn send(&mut self, data: &[u8]) -> Result<(),
String>;

    fn receive(&mut self, buffer: &mut [u8]) ->
Result<usize, String>;

}
```

In the above, we define a trait called NetworkProtocol that includes three methods: connect, send, and receive. Each of these methods takes a mutable reference to self and returns a Result object indicating whether the operation was successful or not.

Implementing a Trait

To implement this trait for a specific type, you use the impl keyword followed by the name of the type and the trait name. For example:

```
struct TcpProtocol {

    // Implementation details

}


impl NetworkProtocol for TcpProtocol {
```

```rust
    fn connect(&mut self, address: &str) -> Result<(),
String> {

        // Implementation for TCP connection

        println!("Connecting to {} via TCP", address);

        Ok(())

    }


    fn send(&mut self, data: &[u8]) -> Result<(), String>
{

        // Implementation for TCP send

        println!("Sending data via TCP: {:?}", data);

        Ok(())

    }


    fn receive(&mut self, buffer: &mut [u8]) ->
Result<usize, String> {

        // Implementation for TCP receive

        println!("Receiving data via TCP");

        Ok(buffer.len())

    }

}
```

In the above implementation, we define a struct called TcpProtocol and implement the
NetworkProtocol trait for it by providing implementations for the connect, send, and receive

methods.

Sample Program: Implementing NetworkProtocol Trait

Once we have implemented the NetworkProtocol trait for one or more types, we can write generic functions and data structures that work with any type implementing the trait. For example, we can define a function that sends a message over the network using any protocol that implements the NetworkProtocol trait:

```rust
fn send_message<T: NetworkProtocol>(protocol: &mut T,
message: &str) -> Result<(), String> {

    let bytes = message.as_bytes();

    protocol.send(bytes)

}


fn main() {

    let mut tcp = TcpProtocol {};

    match tcp.connect("127.0.0.1:8080") {

        Ok(_) => println!("Connected successfully"),

        Err(e) => println!("Failed to connect: {}", e),

    }


    match send_message(&mut tcp, "Hello, World!") {

        Ok(_) => println!("Message sent successfully"),

        Err(e) => println!("Failed to send message: {}",
e),

    }
```

```
}
```

In the above given example,

- The send_message function takes a mutable reference to any type that implements the NetworkProtocol trait, along with a message to send. The function converts the message to a byte array and calls the send method on the protocol.

- The main function creates an instance of TcpProtocol, connects to a server, and sends a message using the send_message function.

Sample Program: Extending for Multiple Protocols

We can extend this concept to work with multiple protocols. For instance, if we want to add a UdpProtocol, we can implement the same trait for it:

```
struct UdpProtocol {

    // Implementation details

}


impl NetworkProtocol for UdpProtocol {

    fn connect(&mut self, address: &str) -> Result<(),
String> {

        // Implementation for UDP connection

        println!("Connecting to {} via UDP", address);

        Ok(())

    }


    fn send(&mut self, data: &[u8]) -> Result<(), String>
{
```

```rust
        // Implementation for UDP send

        println!("Sending data via UDP: {:?}", data);

        Ok(())

    }


    fn receive(&mut self, buffer: &mut [u8]) ->
Result<usize, String> {

        // Implementation for UDP receive

        println!("Receiving data via UDP");

        Ok(buffer.len())

    }

}
```

Now, both TcpProtocol and UdpProtocol can be used interchangeably with the send_message function:

```rust
fn main() {

    let mut tcp = TcpProtocol {};

    let mut udp = UdpProtocol {};


    match tcp.connect("127.0.0.1:8080") {

        Ok(_) => println!("Connected to TCP
successfully"),
```

```rust
        Err(e) => println!("Failed to connect to TCP:
{}", e),
    }


    match send_message(&mut tcp, "Hello, TCP!") {
        Ok(_) => println!("TCP message sent
successfully"),
        Err(e) => println!("Failed to send TCP message:
{}", e),
    }


    match udp.connect("127.0.0.1:8080") {
        Ok(_) => println!("Connected to UDP
successfully"),
        Err(e) => println!("Failed to connect to UDP:
{}", e),
    }


    match send_message(&mut udp, "Hello, UDP!") {
        Ok(_) => println!("UDP message sent
successfully"),
        Err(e) => println!("Failed to send UDP message:
{}", e),
    }
```

```
}
```

Because various protocols can use the same trait, the same code can operate smoothly with all of them.

Error Handling

Overview

Rust provides robust tools to manage errors safely and efficiently knowing that errors can arise from various sources such as network failures, incorrect input/output operations, and unexpected behavior from servers or clients. Rust's error handling mechanisms ensure that programs can handle these issues gracefully, maintaining robustness and clarity in the code.

Error handling in Rust primarily revolves around the Result type, an enum representing either a successful value or an error. This approach mandates explicit error handling, ensuring errors are not accidentally ignored and promoting more reliable and maintainable code.

Result, Ok and Err

The Result type has two variants: Ok and Err. The Ok variant signifies a successful operation and contains the result, while the Err variant signifies an error and contains an error message or type.

Given below is an example of using the Result type for error handling:

```
use std::fs::File;

use std::io::{self, Read};


fn read_file(path: &str) -> Result<String, io::Error> {

    let mut file = File::open(path)?;

    let mut contents = String::new();

    file.read_to_string(&mut contents)?;

    Ok(contents)
```

```
}
```

```
fn main() {

    match read_file("example.txt") {

        Ok(contents) => println!("Contents of file: {}",
contents),

        Err(e) => println!("Error reading file: {}", e),

    }

}
```

In the above given example,

- The read_file function attempts to open a file at the specified path, read its contents into a string, and return the contents as a Result<String, io::Error>.

- The ? operator propagates any errors that occur when opening the file or reading its contents. If the operation succeeds, the function returns an Ok variant containing the file contents. If an error occurs, it returns an Err variant containing a std::io::Error.

- The main function uses pattern matching to handle the returned Result. It prints the file contents if the operation is successful, or the error message if an error occurs.

Panic! Macro

Rust provides the panic! macro for handling unrecoverable errors. When a program encounters an error that cannot be handled or recovered from, it can panic and terminate. Panicking is useful for situations where an unexpected error should not occur during normal operation.

Given below is an example of using the panic! macro:

```
fn divide(x: i32, y: i32) -> i32 {

    if y == 0 {

        panic!("division by zero");
```

```
    }

    x / y
}


fn main() {

    let result = divide(10, 2);

    println!("Result: {}", result);


    let result = divide(10, 0);

    println!("Result: {}", result);

}
```

In the above given example,

- The divide function takes two integers as input and returns their division. If the second argument is zero, the function panics with a message indicating a division by zero error.
- The main function calls the divide function twice: once with valid arguments and once with an invalid argument. When the function panics, the program terminates and prints the error message.

Applying Error Handling

Error handling is essential to ensure that the program can handle unexpected conditions and continue operating smoothly. Following are the some examples of how error handling can be applied in networking:

Handling Connection Errors

```
use std::net::TcpStream;
```

```rust
fn connect_to_server(address: &str) -> Result<TcpStream,
String> {

    match TcpStream::connect(address) {

        Ok(stream) => Ok(stream),

        Err(e) => Err(format!("Failed to connect: {}",
e)),

    }

}


fn main() {

    match connect_to_server("127.0.0.1:8080") {

        Ok(stream) => println!("Connected to server"),

        Err(e) => println!("Error: {}", e),

    }

}
```

In the above given example,

- The connect_to_server function attempts to connect to a server and returns a Result<TcpStream, String>.
- If the connection is successful, it returns an Ok variant with the stream. If an error occurs, it returns an Err variant with an error message.

Handling Data Transmission Errors

```rust
use std::io::{self, Write};

use std::net::TcpStream;
```

```rust
fn send_data(stream: &mut TcpStream, data: &[u8]) ->
Result<(), io::Error> {

    stream.write_all(data)?;

    Ok(())

}


fn main() {

    let mut stream =
TcpStream::connect("127.0.0.1:8080").unwrap();

    match send_data(&mut stream, b"Hello, server!") {

        Ok(_) => println!("Data sent successfully"),

        Err(e) => println!("Failed to send data: {}", e),

    }

}
```

In the above given example,

- The send_data function attempts to send data over a TCP stream and returns a Result<(), io::Error>.

- If the data is sent successfully, it returns an Ok variant. If an error occurs, it returns an Err variant with an io::Error.

Handling Timeout Errors

```rust
use std::io;

use std::net::{TcpStream, ToSocketAddrs};
```

```rust
use std::time::Duration;


fn connect_with_timeout<A: ToSocketAddrs>(address: A) ->
Result<TcpStream, io::Error> {

    let stream =
TcpStream::connect_timeout(&address.to_socket_addrs()?.ne
xt().unwrap(), Duration::new(5, 0))?;

    Ok(stream)

}


fn main() {

    match connect_with_timeout("127.0.0.1:8080") {

        Ok(_) => println!("Connected to server"),

        Err(e) => println!("Failed to connect: {}", e),

    }

}
```

In the above given example,

- The connect_with_timeout function attempts to connect to a server with a timeout and returns a Result<TcpStream, io::Error>.
- If the connection is successful within the timeout, it returns an Ok variant. If an error or timeout occurs, it returns an Err variant with an io::Error.

Summary

In this chapter, we learned several key concepts of Rust programming language that are relevant for network programming. These concepts include mutability, ownership, borrowing, structs, enums, pattern matching, and error handling.

Mutability refers to the ability to change the value of a variable after it has been defined. Rust has a unique approach to mutability in which variables are immutable by default and must be explicitly declared as mutable using the mut keyword. This approach ensures that programs are more reliable and less prone to errors. Ownership is another key concept that is used to manage memory. Rust uses a system of ownership and borrowing to ensure that memory is managed efficiently and that programs are less prone to errors. The ownership system ensures that each piece of data has a unique owner, and that there are no multiple owners for the same data. Borrowing allows multiple parts of a program to access the data without taking ownership of it.

Structs are used to define custom data types. They allow programmers to group related data together and create more complex data structures. Structs can be used to represent various entities in a network, such as a server or a client. Enums are used to define a type with a finite set of possible values. They are commonly used to represent different states or types of messages that can be sent or received. Pattern matching is a powerful feature that allows developers to match the value of an enum against a specific pattern and execute code based on the match. Finally, we learned error handling which is also an essential aspect of network programming which is done using the Result type, which represents either success or failure. We learned how errors can be propagated up the call stack, and code can be written to handle errors in a more effective and efficient manner.

In the next chapter, we will explore and learn various Rust commands and libraries such as std::net library, which provides low-level networking functionality, the tokio library, which is a popular asynchronous runtime for Rust, the hyper library, which is a high-performance HTTP library, the env_logger library, which provides logging functionality, and the reqwest library, which is a simple HTTP client.

CHAPTER 5: RUST COMMANDS FOR NETWORKS

Popular Commands In-Use

Rust provides a robust set of commands for managing and developing projects. These commands, primarily accessed through the command-line interface (CLI), streamline the process of creating, building, managing, and documenting Rust projects. Understanding these commands is crucial for efficient Rust development. This section provides a detailed overview of the essential Rust commands, including their functions and usage.

rustc

The rustc command is the Rust compiler used to compile Rust source code into executable binaries or libraries. It is the fundamental tool that transforms human-readable Rust code into machine code.

```
rustc main.rs
```

This command compiles the main.rs file into an executable named main.

You can specify the output file name using the -o option:

```
rustc main.rs -o my_program
```

To enable optimizations for better performance:

```
rustc -O main.rs
```

To include debug information in the compiled binary:

```
rustc -g main.rs
```

cargo

cargo is Rust's package manager and build system. It simplifies the management of Rust projects by handling dependencies, building projects, and managing project configuration.

- Creating a new project

```
cargo new my_project
```

This command creates a new directory named my_project with the necessary files and directories for a Rust project.

- Building a project

```
cargo build
```

This command compiles the project in the current directory.

- Running a project

```
cargo run
```

This command builds and runs the project, executing its main function.

- Adding dependencies

```
cargo add dependency_name
```

Using the cargo-edit plugin, this command adds a dependency to the Cargo.toml file.

- Updating dependencies

```
cargo update
```

This command updates the dependencies listed in Cargo.lock to the latest versions allowed by the Cargo.toml file.

rustdoc

rustdoc generates documentation from Rust source code. It reads documentation comments in the code and produces HTML documentation.

- Generating documentation

```
rustdoc src/lib.rs
```

This command generates HTML documentation for the lib.rs file in the src directory.

- Viewing documentation

```
cargo doc --open
```

This command generates and opens the documentation for the current project in a web browser.

rustfmt

rustfmt formats Rust code according to the official Rust style guidelines. It helps maintain code consistency and readability across a project.

- Formatting a file

```
rustfmt main.rs
```

- Formatting all files in a project

```
cargo fmt
```

- Checking formatting

```
cargo fmt -- --check
```

This command checks if the code is properly formatted without making changes.

rustup

rustup manages Rust toolchains, allowing the installation and management of multiple versions of the Rust compiler and related tools.

- Installing rust

```
rustup install stable
```

This command installs the stable version of the Rust compiler.

- Switching toolchains

```
rustup default nightly
```

This command switches the default toolchain to the nightly version.

- Updating rust

```
rustup update
```

- Checking installed toolchains

```
rustup toolchain list
```

cargo-edit

cargo-edit is a Cargo plugin used to add, remove, or update dependencies in a Rust project.

- Adding a dependency

```
cargo add serde
```

- Removing a dependency

```
cargo rm serde
```

- Updating a dependency

```
cargo upgrade serde
```

cargo-test

cargo-test compiles and runs tests for a Rust project. It ensures that code changes do not break existing functionality.

- Running all tests

```
cargo test
```

- Running specific tests

```
cargo test test_name
```

- Viewing test output

```
cargo test -- --nocapture
```

cargo-run

cargo-run builds and runs a Rust project. It is particularly useful during development to test changes quickly.

- Passing arguments

```
cargo run -- arg1 arg2
```

This command passes arg1 and arg2 to the program.

Along with rustc for compilation, cargo for project management, rustdoc for documentation, rustfmt for formatting, and rustup for toolchain management, Rust provides a full suite of commands that simplify development. For system-level programming and network applications, Rust's strong command-line ecosystem is just one of many advantages.

std::net Module

The Rust standard library provides the std::net module for network programming. This module contains types and functions for networking, including IP addresses, sockets, and networking protocols. The std::net module is a powerful tool that enables developers to create and manage network connections with ease.

IP Address Types

The std::net module provides several types for representing IP addresses:

- Ipv4Addr: Represents an IPv4 address.
- Ipv6Addr: Represents an IPv6 address.
- IpAddr: An enum that can represent either an IPv4 or IPv6 address.

These above types are essential for working with IP addresses in both the Internet Protocol version 4 (IPv4) and version 6 (IPv6) formats.

Socket Types

The std::net module also provides types for working with sockets:

- TcpStream: Represents a TCP connection.
- TcpListener: Listens for incoming TCP connections.
- UdpSocket: Represents a UDP socket.
- UnixStream: Represents a connection over Unix domain sockets.

These above ones allow you to create and manage network connections using the Transmission

Control Protocol (TCP) and User Datagram Protocol (UDP) protocols.

Sample Program: Using std::net

Below is a sample program demonstrating the use of the std::net module to create a TCP server that listens for incoming connections on a specified port and echoes any data it receives back to the client.

```
use std::io::Read;

use std::io::Write;

use std::net::{TcpListener, TcpStream};


fn handle_client(mut stream: TcpStream) ->
std::io::Result<()> {

    let mut buf = [0; 1024];

    loop {

        let bytes_read = stream.read(&mut buf)?;

        if bytes_read == 0 {

            return Ok(());

        }

        stream.write_all(&buf[..bytes_read])?;

    }

}


fn main() -> std::io::Result<()> {

    let listener = TcpListener::bind("127.0.0.1:8080")?;
```

```
    for stream in listener.incoming() {

        handle_client(stream?)?;

    }

    Ok(())

}
```

In the above sample program,

- The main function creates a TcpListener object that listens for incoming connections on port 8080 of the loopback address (127.0.0.1). The loopback address specifies that the server should only accept connections from the local host.

- The handle_client function takes a TcpStream object that represents a connection to a client and reads data from it in a loop. When data is received, it is echoed back to the client by writing it back to the stream using the write_all method.

- The main function then enters a loop that accepts incoming connections from clients and passes them to the handle_client function for processing. The ? operator is used to propagate any errors that occur during socket operations.

Resolving Hostnames

The std::net module also provides functions for resolving hostnames to IP addresses, such as the lookup_host function. This function returns an iterator over IP addresses for a given hostname.

Following is a sample program demonstrating the use of the lookup_host function to resolve a hostname to an IP address:

```
use std::net::lookup_host;


fn main() -> std::io::Result<()> {

    let hostname = "gitforgits.com";

    for addr in lookup_host(hostname)? {

        println!("{}", addr);
```

```
    }

    Ok(())

}
```

In the above code snippet, the lookup_host function is called with the hostname gitforgits.com. The function returns an iterator over IP addresses for the hostname, which are then printed to the console. No matter how simple or complex your network application is, the std::net module makes it easy to build robust Rust applications.

Tokio: Asynchronous Runtime

Tokio is a powerful runtime designed for writing asynchronous applications. Built on top of the Rust Futures library, Tokio provides an efficient and scalable way to handle asynchronous computations. This makes it an excellent choice for building high-performance network applications, such as servers and clients capable of managing numerous concurrent connections.

Key Abstractions

- Futures: At the heart of Tokio is the concept of a "future", which represents a computation that may not be complete yet. Futures allow you to express asynchronous operations that can be composed and combined, making it easy to build complex asynchronous workflows.

- Reactor: The reactor is responsible for managing I/O resources like sockets and orchestrating the event loop that drives the application. It provides an API for registering interest in I/O events (e.g., data arriving on a socket or a connection closing) and handles these events as they occur.

- Tasks: A task in Tokio is a unit of work scheduled to run on a thread within the Tokio runtime. Tasks can be spawned to manage incoming network connections or to perform asynchronous operations such as reading from or writing to a socket. Tasks can be composed and combined to manage complex operations involving many concurrent connections.

- Utilities for Networking: Tokio offers a rich set of utilities for working with network protocols and transports. For instance, the tokio::net module includes implementations for TCP and UDP, as well as utilities for managing sockets and networking operations. Additionally, Tokio supports other network protocols such as HTTP and WebSockets through its various modules.

Sample Program: Creating TCP using Tokio

Following is a sample program of a simple TCP server written using Tokio:

```rust
use tokio::net::TcpListener;

use tokio::prelude::*;


#[tokio::main]

async fn main() -> Result<(), Box<dyn std::error::Error>>
{

    let mut listener =
TcpListener::bind("127.0.0.1:8080").await?;


    loop {

        let (mut socket, _) = listener.accept().await?;


        tokio::spawn(async move {

            let mut buf = [0; 1024];


            loop {

                let n = socket.read(&mut buf).await?;

                if n == 0 {

                    return Ok(());

                }
```

```
            let s =
std::str::from_utf8(&buf[..n]).unwrap();

            println!("received: {}", s);

        }

    });

    }

}
```

In the above sample program,

- The main function creates a TcpListener that binds to port 8080 on the loopback address (127.0.0.1). This setup listens for incoming TCP connections.

- The program enters an infinite loop where it accepts incoming connections. Each connection spawns a new task to handle the connection.

- The #[tokio::main] attribute macro transforms the main function into an asynchronous function, initializing the Tokio runtime.

- The async and await keywords are used to define asynchronous functions and to wait for asynchronous operations to complete, respectively.

- tokio::spawn is used to spawn a new asynchronous task. Each task can handle a separate connection, allowing the server to handle multiple connections concurrently.

- A fixed-size buffer is used to read data from the socket. The buffer is reused for each read operation, making the code efficient.

With the help of Tokio's abstractions and asynchronous I/O, you can create scalable network apps that can manage any number of connections at once.

Hyper: High-Level HTTP Library

Hyper is a popular HTTP library, offering a high-level abstraction for building HTTP clients and servers. Built on top of the Tokio runtime, Hyper allows for asynchronous and non-blocking I/O operations, making it an excellent choice for high-performance network programming.

Key Features of Hyper

Hyper provides a clean and ergonomic API that is both easy to use and powerful enough to handle complex HTTP scenarios. Some of its key features include:

- Leveraging Tokio's runtime, Hyper supports efficient asynchronous operations.

- Hyper can handle both HTTP/1.x and HTTP/2 protocols.

- It supports streaming large bodies of data and handling multipart form data.

- Hyper allows for the implementation of middlewares to handle logging, compression, and other HTTP-related tasks.

- Through the rustls and openssl crates, Hyper can handle secure connections.

Sample Program: Build HTTP Server using Hyper

Below is a simple example of using Hyper to build an HTTP server that responds with a "Hello, World!" message for every incoming request.

```
use hyper::{Body, Request, Response, Server};

use hyper::rt::Future;

use hyper::service::service_fn_ok;


fn main() {

    // Define a closure that takes a request and returns
a response

    let handler = || {

        service_fn_ok(|req: Request<Body>| {

            // Create a response with a "Hello, World!"
message

            let body = Body::from("Hello, World!");

            Response::new(body)
```

```rust
    })
};


// Create a new HTTP server and bind it to port 3000

let addr = ([127, 0, 0, 1], 3000).into();

let server = Server::bind(&addr)

    .serve(handler)

    .map_err(|e| eprintln!("server error: {}", e));


println!("Listening on http://{}", addr);


// Start the server and run it until it is shut down

hyper::rt::run(server);

}
```

In the above sample program,

- The code imports necessary types and traits from the hyper crate.
- The handler closure is defined to take a Request and return a Response.
- The service_fn_ok function wraps a closure that processes the request and creates a response containing the "Hello, World!" message.
- A Server instance is created and bound to port 3000 on the loopback address (127.0.0.1).
- The server is set to use the defined handler for incoming requests.
- The run method from the hyper::rt module starts the server and keeps it running until it is shut down. This method blocks the current thread, allowing the server to handle requests asynchronously.

Miscellaneous Applications

Hyper's support for asynchronous and non-blocking I/O operations also makes it a suitable choice for building more complex HTTP servers and clients. Following are some advanced features and use cases:

Handling Different Routes

You can use a router or manually match the request paths to handle different routes in your server.

```
let handler = || {

    service_fn_ok(|req: Request<Body>| {

        match (req.method(), req.uri().path()) {

            (&hyper::Method::GET, "/") =>
Response::new(Body::from("Hello, World!")),

            (&hyper::Method::GET, "/health") =>
Response::new(Body::from("OK")),

            _ => Response::new(Body::from("Not Found")),

        }

    })

};
```

Adding Middlewares

Middleware functions can be used for tasks such as logging, authentication, or data compression. Middleware functions wrap around the core request handler.

```
fn log_request(req: Request<Body>) -> Request<Body> {

    println!("Received request: {}", req.uri());

    req

}
```

```
let handler = || {

    service_fn_ok(|req: Request<Body>| {

        let req = log_request(req);

        Response::new(Body::from("Hello, World!"))

    })

};
```

Handling JSON Data

Using the serde crate, you can serialize and deserialize JSON data in requests and responses.

```
#[derive(Serialize, Deserialize)]

struct MyData {

    field1: String,

    field2: i32,

}


let handler = || {

    service_fn_ok(|req: Request<Body>| {

        let data = MyData {

            field1: "value1".to_string(),

            field2: 42,

        };
```

```rust
        let json = serde_json::to_string(&data).unwrap();

        Response::new(Body::from(json))

    })

};
```

Hyper is an effective tool for developing high-performance network applications due to its user-friendly API, compatibility with HTTP/1 and HTTP/2, streaming capabilities, support for middleware, and integration with TLS.

env_logger: Flexible Logging

Overview

env_logger is a Rust crate that provides a flexible logging implementation configurable through environment variables. It is particularly useful in Rust network management for logging information such as network connection status, incoming and outgoing requests, errors, and other significant events. The env_logger crate offers several log levels—trace, debug, info, warn, and error—that allow developers to control the granularity of log output.

Following are the log levels:

- trace: Provides the most detailed logging, useful for tracing the flow of execution.
- debug: Logs detailed information useful for debugging.
- info: Logs informational messages that highlight the progress of the application.
- warn: Logs potentially harmful situations.
- error: Logs error events that might still allow the application to continue running.

Sample Program: Using env_logger

To integrate env_logger into a Rust project, you first need to add it as a dependency in your Cargo.toml file:

```toml
[dependencies]

env_logger = "0.9"
```

Once env_logger is added, you can utilize it in your Rust code. The following example demonstrates how to use env_logger to log information about a network request:

```rust
use std::net::TcpStream;

use std::io::prelude::*;

use std::env;

use env_logger::Env;


fn main() {

    // Configure logger using environment variables


env_logger::from_env(Env::default().default_filter_or("info")).init();


    // Connect to a remote server

    let mut stream =
TcpStream::connect("gitforgits.com:80").unwrap();


    // Send a request to the server

    let request = "GET / HTTP/1.1\r\nHost:
gitforgits.com\r\nConnection: close\r\n\r\n";

    stream.write_all(request.as_bytes()).unwrap();


    // Read the response from the server
```

```
    let mut buffer = [0; 1024];

    stream.read(&mut buffer).unwrap();

    let response = String::from_utf8_lossy(&buffer);


    // Log the response

    info!("Received response: {}", response);

}
```

In the above sample program,

- The env_logger::from_env function sets up the logger to read environment variables to determine the logging level.
- The default_filter_or("info") method specifies the default log level as info if the environment variable is not set.
- The init method initializes the logger.
- A connection to a remote server is established using TcpStream::connect.
- An HTTP GET request is sent to the server.
- The response is read into a buffer and converted to a string.
- The info! macro logs the response. Since the logger is configured to use the info log level, this message will be displayed in the console.

There are various other logging macros as below:

- trace!: Logs detailed tracing information.
- debug!: Logs debugging information.
- warn!: Logs warnings.
- error!: Logs error messages.

Each macro takes a format string and additional arguments, similar to the println! macro.

Customizing env_logger

env_logger supports several customization options, including:

- You can direct logs to a file by configuring the env_logger to use a custom logger that writes to a file.

- Customize the format of log messages by implementing a custom formatting function.

- Filter logs based on their module, enabling finer control over which log messages are displayed.

Following is a quick example of logging to a file:

```rust
use log::info;

use env_logger::{Env, Builder};

use std::fs::File;

use std::io::Write;


fn main() {

    // Open a file for logging

    let log_file = File::create("app.log").unwrap();


    // Configure logger to write to the file

    let mut builder =
Builder::from_env(Env::default().default_filter_or("info"
));


builder.target(env_logger::Target::Pipe(Box::new(log_file
)));

    builder.init();


    info!("This message will be logged to a file.");
```

```
}
```

It is easy to change the log verbosity with env logger since developers can control logging levels through environment variables. The env_logger package offers a lot of flexibility for logging in Rust applications, with features like file logging, custom formats, and module filtering.

reqwest: HTTP Client

reqwest simplifies making HTTP requests with user-friendly APIs. It is built on top of the hyper library, which provides low-level HTTP functionalities. With reqwest, developers can easily send HTTP requests to servers and handle responses efficiently. The library includes features such as handling response bodies, managing cookies, supporting authentication, setting timeouts, and much more.

Key Features of reqwest

- reqwest provides an easy-to-use API for making HTTP requests.
- Built on Tokio, it supports asynchronous I/O operations.
- Capable of handling both HTTP/1.1 and HTTP/2 protocols.
- Built-in support for JSON serialization and deserialization.
- Easily send form data in HTTP requests.
- Support for various authentication mechanisms.
- Configure timeouts and handle HTTP redirects.
- Manage cookies for HTTP sessions.

Sample Program: Making a GET Request to Public API

The following example demonstrates how to use reqwest to make a GET request to a public API and retrieve weather forecast data in JSON format:

To use reqwest, add it to your dependencies in the Cargo.toml file:

```
[dependencies]

reqwest = "0.11.3"

serde = { version = "1.0", features = ["derive"] }
```

```rust
serde_json = "1.0"

tokio = { version = "1", features = ["full"] }


use reqwest::Error;

use serde_json::Value;


#[tokio::main]

async fn main() -> Result<(), Error> {

    let api_key = "YOUR_API_KEY";

    let url =
format!("https://api.openweathermap.org/data/2.5/weather?q=London&appid={}", api_key);

    let response = reqwest::get(&url)

        .await?

        .json::<Value>()

        .await?;


    println!("{:#?}", response);


    Ok(())

}
```

In the above sample program,

- We use the get method to send a GET request to the OpenWeatherMap API with the query parameter q=London and an appid parameter (replace YOUR_API_KEY with your actual API key).

- The await? syntax is used to wait for the response asynchronously.

- The json method parses the response body into a serde_json::Value.

- The parsed JSON response is printed to the console using println!.

Sample Program: Making a POST Request

The following example demonstrates how to send a POST request with a JSON body:

```rust
use reqwest::Error;

use serde::{Serialize, Deserialize};


#[derive(Serialize, Deserialize, Debug)]

struct User {

    name: String,

    age: i32,

}


#[tokio::main]

async fn main() -> Result<(), Error> {

    let user = User {

        name: "John".to_string(),

        age: 30,

    };
```

```rust
    let response = reqwest::Client::new()

        .post("https://httpbin.org/post")

        .json(&user)

        .send()

        .await?

        .text()

        .await?;


    println!("{:#?}", response);


    Ok(())

}
```

In the above sample program,

- A User struct is defined and instantiated.
- The reqwest::Client::new method creates a new HTTP client.
- The post method sends a POST request to https://httpbin.org/post with the user struct serialized into JSON using the json method.
- The send method sends the request, and the text method retrieves the response body as text.
- The response is printed to the console.

As an HTTP client, reqwest simplifies both sending and receiving requests and responses. It supports many features, such as authentication, JSON handling, asynchronous I/O, and more.

Summary

In this chapter, we learned various aspects of network management, including the use of commands and libraries to handle networking. Some of the most popular commands and libraries that we learned include std::net, tokio, hyper, env_logger, and reqwest.

std::net is a standard library that provides networking functionality, including TCP and UDP protocols, socket addressing, and more. We learned the use of the SocketAddr structure to represent socket addresses, as well as the TcpListener and TcpStream types to handle TCP connections. We also learned the use of the tokio library for asynchronous network programming. Tokio is a powerful library that provides a variety of tools for handling asynchronous I/O, including futures, tasks, and streams. We practiced about how to use the tokio::net module to create and manage TCP connections, as well as how to use the tokio::io module to read and write data asynchronously.

Hyper is another popular library for handling network connections in Rust. It is a fast, low-level HTTP library that provides an easy-to-use API for building HTTP clients and servers. We learned how to use the hyper::client module to make HTTP requests and handle responses, as well as how to use the hyper::server module to build HTTP servers. env_logger is a useful library for handling logging in Rust applications, including network applications. We learned how to use env_logger to configure logging, as well as how to use the log crate to generate log messages at different levels of severity.

Finally, we learned about the reqwest library, which is a high-level HTTP client for Rust. We learned how to use the reqwest::Client struct to make HTTP requests and handle responses, as well as how to configure the client to use a specific proxy or SSL certificate. Overall, we learned several popular libraries and commands that can be used to handle network connections, including std::net, tokio, hyper, env_logger, and reqwest.

CHAPTER 6:
PROGRAMMING &
DESIGNING NETWORKS

Up and Running with LAN

Overview

A LAN refers to a group of interconnected devices that are located in a single physical place, like a building, office, or home. A LAN, or local area network, can be as tiny as a single user's home network or as big as a school or office network serving thousands of students or employees. Setting up a Local Area Network (LAN) involves several critical steps to ensure that all devices can communicate effectively. These steps include defining the network topology, assigning IP addresses, and configuring network devices. This chapter covers these steps in detail, providing examples to help you get started with LAN configuration.

Define Network Topology

The network topology refers to the physical and logical arrangement of network devices, including routers, switches, and computers. It also defines the communication paths between these devices.

Graphviz for Network Topology

Graphviz is a powerful tool for visualizing network topologies. It allows you to create diagrams that represent the connections and layout of your network. By using Rust libraries, you can integrate Graphviz to define and visualize your network topology programmatically.

Given below is an example on defining network topology using Graphviz:

```rust
extern crate graphviz;

use graphviz::{Graph, IntoCow};

fn main() {
    // Create a new graph

    let mut graph = Graph::new("network");


    // Add nodes to the graph for the network devices
```

```
let router = graph.add_node("router");

let switch1 = graph.add_node("switch1");

let switch2 = graph.add_node("switch2");

let server = graph.add_node("server");

let client = graph.add_node("client");


// Add edges to the graph for the network connections

graph.add_edge(router, switch1, None);

graph.add_edge(router, switch2, None);

graph.add_edge(switch1, server, None);

graph.add_edge(switch2, client, None);


// Output the graph as a DOT file

println!("{}", graph.into_cow().to_string());

}
```

In the above given example, we create a graph representing a simple network. The nodes represent devices like routers, switches, servers, and clients, while the edges represent the connections between these devices. The resulting graph can be output as a DOT file, which can be visualized using Graphviz tools.

Assign IP Addresses

Each device on a network must have a unique IP address. You can assign IP addresses manually or use Dynamic Host Configuration Protocol (DHCP) to assign them automatically.

Setting up IP Addresses

```rust
use std::net::{Ipv4Addr, SocketAddrV4, TcpListener};

fn main() {
    let ip_address =
"192.168.1.1".parse::<Ipv4Addr>().unwrap();

    let subnet_mask =
"255.255.255.0".parse::<Ipv4Addr>().unwrap();

    let gateway_address =
"192.168.1.254".parse::<Ipv4Addr>().unwrap();

    let port = 8080;

    let socket_addr = SocketAddrV4::new(ip_address,
port);

    let listener =
TcpListener::bind(socket_addr).unwrap();


    println!("IP address: {}", ip_address);

    println!("Subnet mask: {}", subnet_mask);

    println!("Gateway address: {}", gateway_address);

    println!("Listening on: {}",
listener.local_addr().unwrap());

}
```

This Rust program sets up a device with a specific IP address, subnet mask, and gateway address. It also starts a TCP listener on the specified port. You can also adjust the IP address, subnet mask, and gateway address to match your network configuration.

Configure Network Devices

Configuring network devices involves setting various parameters such as IP addresses, subnet masks, default gateways, and DNS servers. This ensures proper communication and routing within the network.

Configure Network Devices using Netlink

Netlink is a messaging system in the Linux kernel that allows user-space processes to communicate with kernel-space processes. The netlink-sys crate provides Rust bindings for the Netlink API, enabling configuration of network devices.

Below is a quick example to configure network devices:

```rust
use netlink_sys::{

    nl_socket_alloc, nl_connect, nl_send_auto,
nlmsg_data, nlmsg_hdr, rtnl_link_get_by_name,

    rtnl_link_ifinfomsg, rtnl_link_info,
rtnl_link_info_data, rtnl_link_set_addr,

    rtnl_link_set_flags, rtnl_link_set_ifname,
rtnl_link_set_ipv4_addr, rtnl_link_set_link,

    rtnl_link_set_mtu, NLMSG_DONE, NLM_F_ACK,
NLM_F_REQUEST, NLM_F_ROOT, NLM_F_ATOMIC,

    NLM_F_CREATE, NLM_F_EXCL, NLM_F_DUMP, NLM_F_REPLACE,
NLM_F_ACK_TLVS, IFF_UP,

};

use std::ffi::CString;

use std::io::{Error, ErrorKind};


fn main() -> Result<(), Error> {

    let mut socket = nl_socket_alloc();
```

```
    if socket.is_null() {

        return Err(Error::new(ErrorKind::Other, "Failed
to allocate netlink socket"));

    }


    if unsafe { nl_connect(socket, 0) } < 0 {

        return Err(Error::new(ErrorKind::Other, "Failed
to connect to netlink socket"));

    }


    let mut link_info = rtnl_link_info {

        n: nlmsg_hdr {

            nlmsg_len: 0,

            nlmsg_type: 0,

            nlmsg_flags: 0,

            nlmsg_seq: 0,

            nlmsg_pid: 0,

        },

        ninfo: rtnl_link_info_data {

            nla_len: 0,

            nla_type: 0,

            nla_data: [0; 0],
```

```rust
        },
    };


    let mut ifindex = 0;

    let ifname = CString::new("eth0").unwrap();

    if unsafe { rtnl_link_get_by_name(socket,
ifname.as_ptr(), &mut link_info) } == 0 {

        ifindex = unsafe {

            nlmsg_data(link_info.n.nh, &mut
rtnl_link_ifinfomsg::new().header as *mut _ as *mut u8)

        }

        .ifi_index;

    }


    if ifindex == 0 {

        return Err(Error::new(ErrorKind::Other, "Failed
to get interface index"));

    }


    let ip_addr = "192.168.1.10";

    let mask = "255.255.255.0";

    let gateway = "192.168.1.1";
```

```rust
    let ip_addr = ip_addr.parse().expect("Invalid IP
address");

    let mask = mask.parse().expect("Invalid subnet
mask");

    let gateway = gateway.parse().expect("Invalid gateway
address");


    if unsafe { rtnl_link_set_ipv4_addr(socket, ifindex,
ip_addr, mask, gateway) } < 0 {

        return Err(Error::new(ErrorKind::Other, "Failed
to set interface IP address"));

    }



    let flags = IFF_UP;

    if unsafe { rtnl_link_set_flags(socket, ifindex,
flags, flags) } < 0 {

        return Err(Error::new(ErrorKind::Other, "Failed
to set interface flags"));

    }



    if unsafe { nl_send_auto(socket, NLMSG_DONE,
NLM_F_ACK | NLM_F_REQUEST) } < 0 {

        return Err(Error::new(ErrorKind::Other, "Failed
to send netlink message"));
```

```
    }


    Ok(())

}
```

This program configures a network interface on a Linux system using the Netlink API. It sets the IP address, subnet mask, and gateway for the interface named eth0, and then brings the interface up by setting the IFF_UP flag.

To run this program, you need to have root privileges. Compile and run the program using the following commands:

```
cargo build
```

```
sudo target/debug/my-program
```

In order to build more advanced network management solutions, it is helpful to first understand how to apply these configurations, and the examples given do just that.

Implementing WAN

WAN Overview

Configuring a Wide Area Network (WAN) is more intricate than setting up a Local Area Network (LAN) due to its broader geographical scope and the need to connect multiple networks. Given below are the broad steps to when configuring a WAN:

- Identify the number of users, the applications and services to be used, and the bandwidth requirements.

- Evaluate technologies such as MPLS, VPN, and leased lines based on cost, performance, reliability, and security.

- Choose a provider that offers the necessary bandwidth and Quality of Service (QoS).

- Set up routers with appropriate routing protocols and security settings to connect different networks.

- Set up physical connections between WAN routers and the service provider's network with proper IP addresses and other settings.

- Implement firewalls, intrusion detection/prevention systems, and encryption to secure the WAN.
- Ensure the WAN functions as expected and optimize settings for better performance and reliability.

WAN Setup Process

- Determining network requirement

The first step involves understanding the network requirements. Assume we need to connect two LAN networks, each with 20 users and requiring a minimum bandwidth of 50Mbps.

- Choose WAN technology

For the below program, we use a VPN (Virtual Private Network) to connect the two LAN networks. VPNs provide secure connections over the internet by encrypting traffic between the networks.

- Select WAN service provider

Choose a third-party VPN service provider that meets the bandwidth and QoS requirements.

- Configure the WAN routers

WAN routers are crucial in connecting different networks and routing traffic between them. We use two routers, one for each LAN network, with both WAN and LAN interfaces. We leverage the actix-web and actix libraries to create a Rust application and OpenVPN to set up the VPN connection.

Sample Program: Configuring WAN Interfaces

First, create a configuration file for the OpenVPN client, "client.conf", containing the VPN server's IP address, port number, and authentication credentials.

Next, configure the WAN interface on each router. Use the actix-web library to create a web server that listens on the WAN interface.

```rust
use actix_web::{web, App, HttpResponse, HttpServer,
Responder};

use std::net::Ipv4Addr;


async fn hello() -> impl Responder {
```

```
        HttpResponse::Ok().body("Hello, world!")

}


#[actix_web::main]

async fn main() -> std::io::Result<()> {

    HttpServer::new(|| {

        App::new()

            .service(web::resource("/").to(hello))

    })

    .bind((Ipv4Addr::new(0, 0, 0, 0), 8080))?

    .run()

    .await

}
```

This code creates a simple web server listening on port 8080 of the WAN interface. Use Ipv4Addr::new() to specify the WAN interface's IP address. For example, one router uses the IP address 192.168.0.1 and the other uses 192.168.0.2.

Configure the WAN Interfaces

The WAN interfaces connect the routers to the service provider's network. Configure these interfaces with appropriate IP addresses, subnet masks, and other settings.

OpenVPN Client Configuration

Create a "client.conf" file for the OpenVPN client. Following is a sample configuration:

```
client

dev tun
```

```
proto udp

remote vpn.gitforgits.com 1194

resolv-retry infinite

nobind

persist-key

persist-tun

ca ca.crt

cert client.crt

key client.key

remote-cert-tls server

cipher AES-256-CBC

verb 3
```

This configuration connects to a VPN server at vpn.gitforgits.com on port 1194 using UDP. It includes paths to the certificate authority file (ca.crt), client certificate (client.crt), and client key (client.key), ensuring secure connections.

Configuring Routers

After setting up the OpenVPN client, configure the WAN interfaces on the routers using Rust and the actix-web library.

```rust
use actix_web::{web, App, HttpResponse, HttpServer,
Responder};

use std::net::Ipv4Addr;


async fn hello() -> impl Responder {
```

```
    HttpResponse::Ok().body("Hello, world!")

}


#[actix_web::main]

async fn main() -> std::io::Result<()> {

    HttpServer::new(|| {

        App::new()

            .service(web::resource("/").to(hello))

    })

    .bind((Ipv4Addr::new(192, 168, 0, 1), 8080))?

    .run()

    .await

}
```

The web server listens on the WAN interface at 192.168.0.1:8080.

After configuring the WAN, test it to ensure it works as expected. Use network testing tools to measure performance, latency, and packet loss.

Testing WAN

Use tools like iperf to measure network performance and ping to test connectivity between the networks.

```
iperf -c <WAN_IP> -p 8080 -t 60

ping <WAN_IP>
```

These commands measure network performance and test connectivity, helping identify and resolve potential issues.

Finding out what the network needs, picking out a service provider, configuring interfaces and routers, establishing security, and testing the network are all part of the process of configuring a WAN.

WLAN into Action

WLAN Setup

Configuring a Wireless Local Area Network (WLAN) involves several steps to ensure proper installation, security, and functionality. Below are the broad steps to configure a WLAN:

- Determine the coverage area, the number and placement of access points, and the type of wireless equipment needed.

- Mount the access points, connect them to the wired network, and configure network settings such as SSID, channel, and transmit power.

- Implement security protocols like WPA2, enable MAC filtering, guest access, and VPNs to prevent unauthorized access and data theft.

- Set up wireless network settings on client devices, including SSID, security type, and password.

- Connect client devices and test data transfer, network performance, and security features.

- Monitor for performance issues, security breaches, and other problems, and troubleshoot as necessary.

Sample Program: End-to-End Setup of a WLAN

Setting up a WLAN using Rust involves configuring access points, securing the network, and connecting client devices. Below are detailed steps and code examples to achieve this.

Install Necessary Libraries

First, install the necessary libraries for interfacing with the operating system's networking functions. The wifi crate can be used for this purpose. Install it using the following command:

```
cargo install wifi
```

Setup Access Points

Use the wifi::interface module to retrieve the list of available wireless interfaces, scan for available access points, and select one to connect to. Below is a sample Rust code to do this:

```rust
use wifi::scan;

use wifi::interface::get;

use wifi::config::Open;


fn main() {

    let iface = get("wlan0").unwrap();

    let ap_list = scan(&iface).unwrap();


    for ap in ap_list {

        println!("SSID: {}\tSignal: {}\tChannel: {}",
ap.ssid, ap.signal, ap.channel);

    }


    let selected_ap = &ap_list[0];

    iface.connect(&selected_ap, &Open, None).unwrap();

}
```

In the code above, we:

- Retrieve the wlan0 interface using the get function.
- Scan for available access points using the scan function and print the list of detected access points.
- Select the first access point from the list and connect to it using the connect method.

Configure Security

WLAN security is also equally critical to prevent unauthorized access and network attacks. Below is how we configure WPA2 security:

```
use wifi::security::wpa::{Config, Password};


fn main() {
    let iface = get("wlan0").unwrap();

    let ap_list = scan(&iface).unwrap();

    let selected_ap = &ap_list[0];


    let psk = Password::from("mysecretpassword");

    let config = Config::from_psk(&psk);


    iface.connect(&selected_ap, &config, None).unwrap();
}
```

In the code above, we:

- Define a password for WPA2 security using the Password::from method.
- Create a WPA2 configuration using the Config::from_psk method.
- Connect to the selected access point using the connect method with the WPA2 configuration.

Configure Client Devices

Configure client devices to connect to the WLAN by setting up wireless network settings on the device. Below is how we configure a client device:

```
use wifi::client::{Client, Security};
```

```
fn main() {

    let ssid = "mywifinetwork";

    let password = "mysecretpassword";

    let security = Security::Wpa2Personal { password:
password.into() };


    let client = Client::new();

    client.connect(ssid, security).unwrap();

}
```

In the code above, we:

- Define the SSID and password for the WLAN network.
- Create a security configuration using the Security::Wpa2Personal method with the password.
- Create a new Client instance and connect to the WLAN using the connect method with the SSID and security configuration.

Test WLAN

And, now to test the WLAN, connect client devices and perform data transfer, network performance, and security feature tests. Below is a sample Rust code to test the WLAN:

```
use wifi::client::{Client, Security};


fn main() {

    let ssid = "mywifinetwork";

    let password = "mysecretpassword";
```

```rust
    let security = Security::Wpa2Personal { password:
password.into() };


    let client = Client::new();

    match client.connect(ssid, security) {

        Ok(_) => println!("Connected to WLAN"),

        Err(e) => println!("Failed to connect: {}", e),

    }

}
```

In the code above, we attempt to connect to the WLAN and print whether the connection was successful or not.

Monitoring WLAN

Monitoring the WLAN involves checking for performance issues, security breaches, and other problems and for this tools like ping and iperf which we have used in the previous chapter can be used for this purpose.

Let us take a look at the below example on monitoring using ping:

```rust
use std::process::Command;


fn main() {

    let output = Command::new("ping")

        .arg("-c 4")

        .arg("192.168.1.1")

        .output()
```

```
    .expect("Failed to execute command");


    println!("Ping output: {}",
String::from_utf8_lossy(&output.stdout));

}
```

In the above given example, we use the ping command to check connectivity to a specific IP address and print the output. The same way we can do using iperf wherein we install iperf on our system and run the following Rust code to check network performance as below:

```
use std::process::Command;


fn main() {

    let output = Command::new("iperf3")

        .arg("-c")

        .arg("192.168.1.1")

        .output()

        .expect("Failed to execute command");


    println!("iperf3 output: {}",
String::from_utf8_lossy(&output.stdout));

}
```

In the above, we use the iperf3 command to check network performance to a specific IP address and print the output.

All things considered, there are a number of steps involved in configuring a WLAN, such as planning the deployment, installing access points, configuring security, configuring client devices, testing the network, and keeping an eye out for problems.

Getting Started with Cloud Networks

Overview

Configuring a cloud network involves several steps to ensure proper setup, security, and functionality. Below is a quick overview on the steps to configure cloud networks:

- Select AWS, Microsoft Azure, or Google Cloud.

- Define the IP address range, create subnets, and configure security groups within the VPC.

- Set up internet gateways, NAT gateways, VPN connections, and routing tables.

- Deploy virtual machines, databases, and other services within the VPC.

- Use either of the cloud provider tools to monitor network traffic, view logs, and set up alerts. Manage network resources and update configurations as needed.

Sample Program: Setting up AWS Cloud Network

We will use AWS and the Rust SDK, rusoto, to create a VPC, configure network access, launch resources, and monitor the network.

Setup AWS Credentials

First, set up the AWS credentials. You can do this by creating a configuration file in the .aws directory in your home folder. Create two files, config and credentials.

In the config file:

```
[default]

region=us-west-2
```

And, in the credentials file:

```
[default]

aws_access_key_id=YOUR_ACCESS_KEY

aws_secret_access_key=YOUR_SECRET_KEY
```

Replace YOUR_ACCESS_KEY and YOUR_SECRET_KEY with your actual AWS access key and secret key.

Create a VPC

Use the following code snippet using the rusoto crate to create a VPC:

```
use rusoto_core::Region;

use rusoto_ec2::{Ec2, Ec2Client, CreateVpcRequest};


fn create_vpc() {
    let client = Ec2Client::new(Region::UsWest2);


    let vpc_req = CreateVpcRequest {
        cidr_block: "10.0.0.0/16".to_string(),
        instance_tenancy: Some("default".to_string()),
        ..Default::default()
    };


    match client.create_vpc(vpc_req).sync() {
        Ok(resp) => {
            let vpc_id =
resp.vpc.unwrap().vpc_id.unwrap();
            println!("VPC created with ID: {}", vpc_id);
        }
```

```
        Err(e) => panic!("Error creating VPC: {:?}", e),

    }

}
```

This code creates a VPC with the CIDR block 10.0.0.0/16 and default instance tenancy, and prints the VPC ID.

Configure Network Access

Next, configure network access by setting up an internet gateway and attaching it to the VPC.

- Create an Internet Gateway

```
use rusoto_ec2::{CreateInternetGatewayRequest, Ec2};


fn create_internet_gateway() {

    let client = Ec2Client::new(Region::UsWest2);


    let igw_req = CreateInternetGatewayRequest {

        ..Default::default()

    };


    match client.create_internet_gateway(igw_req).sync()
{

        Ok(resp) => {

            let igw_id =
resp.internet_gateway.unwrap().internet_gateway_id.unwrap
();
```

```rust
        println!("Internet gateway created with ID: {}", igw_id);

        }

        Err(e) => panic!("Error creating internet gateway: {:?}", e),

    }

}
```

- Attach the Internet Gateway to the VPC:

```rust
use rusoto_ec2::{AttachInternetGatewayRequest, Ec2};


fn attach_internet_gateway(vpc_id: &str, igw_id: &str) {

    let client = Ec2Client::new(Region::UsWest2);


    let attach_req = AttachInternetGatewayRequest {

        vpc_id: vpc_id.to_string(),

        internet_gateway_id: igw_id.to_string(),

    };


    match client.attach_internet_gateway(attach_req).sync() {

        Ok(_) => println!("Internet gateway attached to VPC"),
```

```
        Err(e) => panic!("Error attaching internet
gateway: {:?}", e),

    }

}
```

Configure Firewall Rules

Set up security rules for the cloud network using AWS Security Groups. Below is a sample code to create a security group and add rules:

```
use rusoto_ec2::{CreateSecurityGroupRequest,
AuthorizeSecurityGroupIngressRequest, IpPermission, Ec2};


fn create_security_group(vpc_id: &str) -> String {

    let client = Ec2Client::new(Region::UsWest2);


    let sg_req = CreateSecurityGroupRequest {

        group_name: "my-security-group".to_string(),

        description: "My security group".to_string(),

        vpc_id: Some(vpc_id.to_string()),

        ..Default::default()

    };


    let sg_id = match
client.create_security_group(sg_req).sync() {

        Ok(resp) => resp.group_id.unwrap(),
```

```rust
        Err(e) => panic!("Error creating security group:
{:?}", e),

    };


    let ip_permission = IpPermission {

        ip_protocol: Some("tcp".to_string()),

        from_port: Some(22),

        to_port: Some(22),

        ip_ranges: Some(vec!["0.0.0.0/0".to_string()]),

        ..Default::default()

    };


    let auth_req = AuthorizeSecurityGroupIngressRequest {

        group_id: Some(sg_id.clone()),

        ip_permissions: Some(vec![ip_permission]),

        ..Default::default()

    };


    match
client.authorize_security_group_ingress(auth_req).sync()
{

        Ok(_) => println!("Ingress rule added to security
group"),
```

```
        Err(e) => panic!("Error adding ingress rule:
{:?}", e),

    };


    sg_id

}
```

This code creates a security group and adds an ingress rule to allow SSH access on port 22 from any IP address.

Launch Instances

Launch instances within the VPC using the AWS EC2 API:

```rust
use rusoto_ec2::{RunInstancesRequest, TagSpecification,
Ec2};


fn launch_instance(subnet_id: &str, sg_id: &str) {

    let client = Ec2Client::new(Region::UsWest2);


    let run_req = RunInstancesRequest {

        image_id: Some("ami-
0c55b159cbfafe1f0".to_string()), // Use an appropriate
AMI ID

        instance_type: Some("t2.micro".to_string()),

        max_count: 1,

        min_count: 1,
```

```rust
        subnet_id: Some(subnet_id.to_string()),

        security_group_ids:
Some(vec![sg_id.to_string()]),

        tag_specifications: Some(vec![TagSpecification {

            resource_type: Some("instance".to_string()),

            tags: Some(vec![("Name".to_string(), "my-
instance".to_string())]),

        }]),

        ..Default::default()

    };


    match client.run_instances(run_req).sync() {

        Ok(resp) => {

            let instance_id =
resp.instances.unwrap()[0].instance_id.clone().unwrap();

            println!("Instance launched with ID: {}",
instance_id);

        }

        Err(e) => panic!("Error launching instance:
{:?}", e),

    }

}
```

This code launches an EC2 instance in the specified subnet with the provided security group.

Setup Load Balancers

Set up load balancers to distribute traffic across multiple instances:

```rust
use rusoto_elbv2::{CreateLoadBalancerRequest,
CreateTargetGroupRequest, Elb, ElbClient};


fn create_load_balancer(vpc_id: &str) {
    let client = ElbClient::new(Region::UsWest2);


    let lb_req = CreateLoadBalancerRequest {

        name: "my-load-balancer".to_string(),

        subnets: vec![vpc_id.to_string()],

        ..Default::default()
    };


    match client.create_load_balancer(lb_req).sync() {

        Ok(resp) => {

            let lb_arn =
resp.load_balancers.unwrap()[0].load_balancer_arn.clone()
.unwrap();

            println!("Load balancer created with ARN:
{}", lb_arn);

        }
```

```
        Err(e) => panic!("Error creating load balancer:
{:?}", e),

    }

}
```

This code creates a load balancer within the specified VPC.

Configure Monitoring and Alerts

To set up monitoring and alerts, tool like Prometheus is the best fit. Below is a basic setup for monitoring using Prometheus:

To begin, first download and install Prometheus from the official website. Then, edit the prometheus.yml file to add your targets. And, then start Prometheus using the following command:

```
./prometheus --config.file=prometheus.yml
```

A cloud network must be configured in several stages, including creating a VPC, configuring network access, launching resources, establishing security rules, configuring monitoring and alerts, and managing the network. You can build and manage a cloud network with ease using AWS and the Rust software development kit (rusoto), guaranteeing a secure and dependable cloud infrastructure for your applications.

Configure VPN

Overview

Lets move to configuring a VPN which involves several stages to ensure secure and efficient connectivity between devices or networks. Below are the straightforward steps to configure a VPN successfully.

Now, setting up a VPN also involves multiple steps including choosing the VPN protocol, configuring the server, setting up user accounts, and configuring client devices. Below is a quick way of setting up a VPN using the OpenVPN protocol.

- To begin with, we will set up a client-to-site VPN using the OpenVPN protocol.
- We will use a cloud-based VPN server on AWS.
- Install and configure OpenVPN Access Server on an Ubuntu 20.04 AWS EC2 instance.

- Then, we launch an EC2 instance on AWS

```
ssh -i "your-key.pem" ubuntu@ec2-public-dns.amazonaws.com
```

- Update the server and install OpenVPN

```
sudo apt-get update

sudo apt-get upgrade

sudo apt-get install openvpn
```

- Install OpenVPN Access Server

```
wget https://swupdate.openvpn.net/as/openvpn-as-2.8.7-
Ubuntu20.amd_64.deb

sudo dpkg -i openvpn-as-2.8.7-Ubuntu20.amd_64.deb
```

- Open a web browser and navigate to https://<public_ip_address>:943/admin. Follow the prompts to set up the server, including creating an administrator account and configuring network settings.
- Download the client software from the OpenVPN Access Server web interface and install it on client devices.
- Set up user accounts for VPN access via the OpenVPN Access Server web interface:
  - Navigate to the "User Permissions" section.
  - Add users and configure permissions.
- Verify the VPN connection
- Connect to the VPN using a client device.
- Ensure that the connection is secure and stable.
- Verify access to network resources.

Sample Program: VPN Configuration

Following is an example of a Rust application for setting up a VPN using the OpenVPN protocol:

- Install necessary Rust libraries

```
cargo install openvpn
```

- Create a Rust program to configure the VPN server

```rust
use std::process::Command;


fn main() {

    // Update and install necessary packages

    Command::new("sh")

        .arg("-c")

        .arg("sudo apt-get update && sudo apt-get upgrade
-y && sudo apt-get install -y openvpn")

        .status()

        .expect("Failed to update and install packages");


    // Download and install OpenVPN Access Server

    Command::new("sh")

        .arg("-c")

        .arg("wget
https://swupdate.openvpn.net/as/openvpn-as-2.8.7-
Ubuntu20.amd_64.deb && sudo dpkg -i openvpn-as-2.8.7-
Ubuntu20.amd_64.deb")

        .status()

        .expect("Failed to download and install OpenVPN
Access Server");
```

```
    println!("OpenVPN Access Server installed. Please
configure it via the web interface at
https://<public_ip_address>:943/admin");

}
```

- Set up user accounts and configure the VPN server via the web interface.
- Then, configure client devices using the downloaded configuration file from the OpenVPN Access Server.
- And finally, you can monitor and maintain the VPN using prometheus.

By following these above well detailed steps, you can set up a VPN ensuring secure and efficient connectivity for your network is well established using simple rust scripting.

Setting up Data Center Network

Overview

Setting up a data center network involves various complex tasks and steps. The following are the detailed steps that can be taken to set up a data center network:

- Determine the requirements for the data center network, including the number of servers, switches, routers, and other networking devices that will be needed.
- Once the network architecture has been planned, select the appropriate networking devices. This includes switches, routers, firewalls, load balancers, and other devices.
- Configure the devices to meet the requirements of the data center network. This includes setting up VLANs, creating access control lists, and configuring routing protocols.
- Enable the creation of virtual machines hosted on physical servers using virtualization software such as VMware, Hyper-V, or KVM.
- Set up storage area networks (SANs) and network-attached storage (NAS) to manage data storage needs.
- Set up firewalls, intrusion prevention systems, and other security devices to protect the data center network from cyber threats.
- Use network monitoring tools, performance monitoring tools, and configuration management tools to manage the data center network.

- Verify that the network is working correctly by testing for performance, security, and reliability.
- Regularly apply security patches, update firmware, and upgrade hardware and software to ensure the network continues to meet organizational requirements.

Sample Program: Setting up a Data Center Network

In the below Rust program, we will assume that we have a data center with two racks of servers that need to be connected to a central switch. We will use the Rust networking library, Tokio, to build our program.

- Import Required Libraries

```
use tokio::net::{TcpListener, TcpStream};

use tokio::io::{AsyncReadExt, AsyncWriteExt};

use std::net::SocketAddr;
```

- Define Network Topology

```
let server1: SocketAddr =
"192.168.1.1:8000".parse().unwrap();

let server2: SocketAddr =
"192.168.1.2:8000".parse().unwrap();

let switch: SocketAddr =
"192.168.1.3:8000".parse().unwrap();
```

- Configure Network Devices

```
let mut switch_listener =
TcpListener::bind(switch).await.unwrap();


// Connect server1 to switch
```

```rust
let mut server1_stream =
TcpStream::connect(switch).await.unwrap();

let mut server1_buf = [0; 1024];

let (mut server1_reader, mut server1_writer) =
server1_stream.split();


// Connect server2 to switch

let mut server2_stream =
TcpStream::connect(switch).await.unwrap();

let mut server2_buf = [0; 1024];

let (mut server2_reader, mut server2_writer) =
server2_stream.split();


// Listen for incoming connections on switch

let (mut switch_stream, _) =
switch_listener.accept().await.unwrap();

let mut switch_buf = [0; 1024];

let (mut switch_reader, mut switch_writer) =
switch_stream.split();
```

- Test the Network

```rust
// Send a message from server1 to server2

server1_writer.write_all(b"Hello,
server2!").await.unwrap();
```

```
server1_writer.flush().await.unwrap();


// Read the message on server2

server2_reader.read(&mut server2_buf).await.unwrap();

println!("Server2 received: {:?}", &server2_buf[..]);


// Send a message from server2 to server1

server2_writer.write_all(b"Hello,
server1!").await.unwrap();

server2_writer.flush().await.unwrap();
```

By following these above steps, you can ensure that your data center network is functioning as expected and can provide the necessary support for the applications running on it.

Summary

In this chapter, we learned how to configure various types of networks using the Rust programming language and its libraries. We started with an overview of the network design process, which involves determining the physical and logical layout of the network, including the placement of routers, switches, and other networking devices. We then learned how to set up an IP address using Rust programming and libraries, including defining the IP addressing scheme and creating a Rust program to set up an IP address in a LAN network. We also explored how to configure network devices, such as routers and switches, using Rust programming and libraries, with an example Rust program.

We then moved on to configuring WAN networks, WLAN networks, cloud networks, VPNs, and data center networks. For each type of network, we provided a detailed step-by-step practical walkthrough to follow in order to successfully establish and configure the networks. Finally, we learned the importance of testing the network to ensure it is functioning as expected. We provided steps for testing connectivity between devices, measuring bandwidth and latency, testing failover and redundancy, testing security, and monitoring the network.

CHAPTER 7:
ESTABLISHING &
MANAGING NETWORK
PROTOCOLS

Introduction to TCP/IP

The TCP/IP protocol suite forms the backbone of modern network communication, enabling devices to interact seamlessly over the internet. Standing for Transmission Control Protocol/Internet Protocol, TCP/IP is not a single protocol but a suite of communication protocols that work together to ensure data is transmitted reliably and efficiently across networks.

Overview

TCP/IP is organized into a layered architecture, with each layer responsible for specific network functions. This modular design allows for flexibility and scalability in network communications.

Application Layer

The application layer is the topmost layer where user applications and network services reside. This layer provides protocols for various data communication services, such as HTTP (used for web browsing), FTP (used for file transfers), SMTP (used for sending emails), and DNS (used for domain name resolution). These protocols define the rules for how applications on different devices can communicate over the network.

Transport Layer

The transport layer is crucial for end-to-end communication. It ensures that data is transferred reliably and accurately between devices. Two primary protocols operate at this layer:

- Transmission Control Protocol (TCP): TCP is connection-oriented, meaning it establishes a connection before transmitting data. It ensures data integrity by providing mechanisms for error-checking and retransmission of lost packets. TCP guarantees that data arrives in the same order it was sent, making it ideal for applications where reliability is critical, such as web browsing and email.

- User Datagram Protocol (UDP): Unlike TCP, UDP is connectionless and does not guarantee the delivery of packets. It is faster and more efficient for applications where speed is more critical than reliability, such as live streaming and online gaming.

Internet Layer

The internet layer is responsible for packet routing across networks. The key protocol at this layer is the Internet Protocol (IP), which handles the addressing and routing of packets to ensure they reach their intended destination. IP defines the format of packets and the addressing scheme (IPv4 or IPv6). Additional protocols like ICMP (used for error messages and network diagnostics) and ARP (used to map IP addresses to MAC addresses) also operate at this layer.

Link Layer (Network Interface Layer)

The link layer deals with the physical transmission of data over network media. It encompasses the protocols and standards that manage data exchange between network devices on the same local network. Ethernet and Wi-Fi are common link layer technologies. This layer is responsible for framing data packets and handling error detection and correction for data that traverses physical media.

Key Concepts in TCP/IP

IP Addressing

Every device on a network is assigned a unique IP address, which serves as its identifier for routing data. IPv4 addresses are 32-bit numbers (e.g., 192.168.1.1), while IPv6 addresses are 128-bit numbers (e.g., 2001:0db8:85a3:0000:0000:8a2e:0370:7334). IP addresses are critical for directing packets to their correct destinations.

Subnetting

Subnetting divides a large network into smaller, more manageable subnetworks. This improves routing efficiency and enhances security by isolating different network segments. A subnet mask (e.g., 255.255.255.0) is used to identify the network and host portions of an IP address.

Routing

Routers are devices that direct data packets between networks. They determine the best path for data to travel from the source to the destination. Routing protocols, such as OSPF (Open Shortest Path First) and BGP (Border Gateway Protocol), help routers dynamically find the optimal path for data packets.

TCP Connection Establishment

Establishing a TCP connection involves a process known as the three-way handshake:

- SYN (Synchronize): The client sends a synchronization packet to the server.

- SYN-ACK (Synchronize-Acknowledge): The server responds with a synchronization acknowledgment packet.

- ACK (Acknowledge): The client sends an acknowledgment packet back to the server, establishing the connection. This process ensures both the client and server are ready for data transmission.

Data Encapsulation

As data moves down the layers of the TCP/IP model, it is encapsulated with the necessary protocol information. For instance, an application layer message is encapsulated in a transport layer segment, which is then encapsulated in an IP packet, and finally in a link layer frame. This encapsulation process allows each layer to add its own control information to the data.

Advantages of TCP/IP

TCP/IP has several key advantages that have made it the dominant protocol suite for network communications:

- TCP/IP allows diverse network devices from different manufacturers to communicate seamlessly, fostering a high degree of interoperability and standardization across the internet.

- The hierarchical nature of IP addressing and the use of subnetting enable networks to scale efficiently, accommodating a vast number of devices and supporting extensive networks without significant performance degradation.

- TCP/IP is designed to operate over various physical networks and to handle a wide range of traffic patterns and requirements. Its robustness ensures reliable data transmission even in complex network environments.

- The protocols within the TCP/IP suite are designed to handle errors and recover from failures gracefully. Mechanisms for error detection, correction, and retransmission ensure data integrity and reliability.

Modern network communication relies on the TCP/IP protocol suite, which allows for scalable, adaptable, and dependable data transmission over networks like the internet. Acquiring familiarity with its layered architecture, essential concepts, and numerous applications provides a strong grounding for handling network communications in different settings.

Port Selection in TCP/IP Protocol

Selecting an appropriate port number is a crucial step in setting up a TCP/IP protocol. Ports act as communication endpoints identified by numbers ranging from 0 to 65535. When an application establishes a network connection, it specifies a port number to communicate with other devices. Ensuring the chosen port number is unique and appropriate prevents conflicts with other applications on the same machine or network.

Allocation of Port Numbers

The Internet Assigned Numbers Authority (IANA) manages and allocates port numbers for specific protocols. These port numbers fall into three categories:

Well-Known Ports (0-1023)

These ports are reserved for specific protocols and widely used by standard services and applications. Following are some of the examples:

- Port 80: Hypertext Transfer Protocol (HTTP)

- Port 443: Hypertext Transfer Protocol Secure (HTTPS)

- Port 25: Simple Mail Transfer Protocol (SMTP)

- Port 21: File Transfer Protocol (FTP)

- Port 22: Secure Shell (SSH)

- Port 23: Telnet

- Port 53: Domain Name System (DNS)

- Port 110: Post Office Protocol version 3 (POP3)

- Port 143: Internet Message Access Protocol version 4 (IMAP4)

- Port 3389: Remote Desktop Protocol (RDP)

Using these well-known ports for their intended purposes ensures compatibility and avoids conflicts with other applications. For instance, web servers typically use port 80 or 443 for HTTP or HTTPS communication, while email servers use port 25 for SMTP.

Registered Ports (1024-49151)

These ports are assigned by IANA for specific services and applications that are not as widely known as those using well-known ports. Registered ports cater to specialized services such as database management systems or network backup solutions. For example:

- Port 1433: Microsoft SQL Server

- Port 3306: MySQL Database

- Port 8080: Alternative HTTP port, often used for web proxies and caching servers

Registered ports provide a balance between avoiding conflicts and ensuring that specialized services have a predictable port number.

Dynamic/Private Ports (49152-65535)

These ports are used by applications for temporary communication needs and are assigned dynamically by the operating system. Dynamic ports are suitable for client-side communication where the port number does not need to be fixed. When an application connects to a remote device, the operating system selects an available port from this range.

Application-Wise Port Selection

When choosing a port number for your application, consider the application's usage context and network environment:

Single-User or Private Network Applications

For applications used by a single user or within a private network, select a port number that is not well-known and unlikely to conflict with other applications. For example, if you develop an internal tool for your organization, using a port number in the registered or dynamic range might be appropriate to avoid conflicts with standard services.

Public Network Applications

If your application is designed for use on a public network, choose a well-known port number that aligns with the type of communication your application provides. For instance, if you are developing a web server application, using port 80 or 443 for HTTP or HTTPS ensures compatibility and ease of use for clients.

While choosing port number, ensuring you are considering following factors:

1. Ensure the chosen port number does not conflict with other services running on the same machine. Tools like netstat or ss can help check active port usage on a system.

2. Use non-default ports for services when possible to reduce the risk of targeted attacks. However, relying solely on obscure port numbers for security is not advisable; robust security measures such as firewalls and encryption should be implemented.

3. Adhere to network policies and guidelines when selecting port numbers, especially in corporate or institutional environments where certain ports might be restricted or monitored.

Generally speaking, when choosing ports, it's best to stay away from popular ones for non-standard services, follow all network policies, and put strong security measures in place. Reliability and efficiency in networked applications are improvised by this meticulous planning and consideration.

Up and Running with Networking Libraries

In this section, we will learn two primary networking libraries: Mio and Rust-Async. These libraries enable developers to build efficient, non-blocking network applications. By the end of this section, you will understand what these libraries are, their core functionalities, and how to install and configure them in your existing Rust environment.

Introduction to Mio

Mio (Metal IO) is a low-level, asynchronous I/O library for Rust that provides non-blocking, event-driven APIs for handling network and other I/O operations. It serves as a foundation for building high-performance network applications and is often used to build more complex frameworks and libraries.

Following are the key features of Mio:

- Mio is built around the concept of event-driven programming, where the application reacts to events such as incoming data or connection requests.

- Mio provides non-blocking I/O operations, allowing your application to handle multiple connections simultaneously without being blocked by any single operation.

- Mio supports multiple platforms, including Linux, macOS, and Windows, making it versatile for cross-platform network applications.

Installing and Configuring Mio

To get started with Mio, you need to add it to your project. Open your Cargo.toml file and add Mio as a dependency:

```
[dependencies]

mio = "0.8"
```

Next, you can create a basic Mio application. Following is a simple example that sets up a TCP listener:

```
use mio::{Events, Interest, Poll, Token};

use mio::net::TcpListener;

use std::io;

use std::net::SocketAddr;


fn main() -> io::Result<()> {

    // Create a poll instance

    let mut poll = Poll::new()?;


    // Create storage for events
```

```rust
    let mut events = Events::with_capacity(128);

    // Define a token to identify the listener
    const SERVER: Token = Token(0);

    // Create a TCP listener
    let addr: SocketAddr =
"127.0.0.1:8080".parse().unwrap();

    let mut listener = TcpListener::bind(addr)?;

    // Register the listener with the poll instance
    poll.registry().register(&mut listener, SERVER,
Interest::READABLE)?;

    // Event loop
    loop {
        // Poll for events
        poll.poll(&mut events, None)?;

        // Process events
        for event in &events {
            if event.token() == SERVER {
```

```
                    // Accept and handle new connections

                    while let Ok((mut socket, _)) =
listener.accept() {

                        println!("New connection
established");

                        // Handle the socket

                    }

                }

            }

        }

    }
```

In the above configuration,

- A Poll instance is created to monitor events.
- A TcpListener is set up to listen for incoming TCP connections.
- The listener is registered with the poll instance to be notified of readable events.
- An event loop is implemented to poll for and handle events.

Introduction to Rust-Async

Rust-Async is a collection of libraries and tools for writing asynchronous code. It leverages Rust's powerful async/await syntax to make asynchronous programming more intuitive and less error-prone. While Tokio is the most popular runtime for async programming, other libraries like async-std and futures also play significant roles in the async ecosystem.

Following are the key features of Rust-Async:

- Simplifies writing and reading asynchronous code, making it easier to understand and maintain.
- Allows writing concurrent code that can perform multiple tasks simultaneously without blocking the main thread.
- Integrates well with existing Rust libraries and tools, providing a seamless development

experience.

Installing and Configuring Rust-Async

To get started with Rust-Async, particularly using async-std, add it to your Cargo.toml file:

```
[dependencies]

async-std = "1.10"
```

Following is an example that sets up a TCP server using async-std:

```
use async_std::task;

use async_std::net::{TcpListener, TcpStream};

use std::io;


async fn handle_client(mut stream: TcpStream) ->
io::Result<()> {

    let mut buffer = [0; 1024];

    let n = stream.read(&mut buffer).await?;

    stream.write_all(&buffer[0..n]).await?;

    Ok(())

}


#[async_std::main]

async fn main() -> io::Result<()> {

    let listener =
TcpListener::bind("127.0.0.1:8080").await?;
```

```
    println!("Server listening on 127.0.0.1:8080");


    while let Ok((stream, _)) = listener.accept().await {

        task::spawn(handle_client(stream));

    }


    Ok(())

}
```

In the above given example,

- An async function handle_client reads from and writes to a TCP stream.
- The main function is annotated with #[async_std::main] to enable async/await.
- A TcpListener listen for incoming connections, which are handled concurrently using task::spawn.

Just to summarize, Mio is best suited for low-level, event-driven network programming and very much ideal for custom implementations requiring fine-grained control over I/O operations. Whereas, Rust-Async aims to simplify asynchronous programming with async/await syntax and is considered to be suitable for high-level, concurrent network applications.

Creating TCP Listener/Binding Socket

Overview

A TCP listener is essentially a server that waits for incoming network connections on a specified port. When a connection request arrives, the listener accepts the connection and creates a new socket to handle communication with the remote client.

Binding a socket refers to associating a socket with a specific IP address and port number. This allows the operating system to route incoming network connections to the correct application. The IP address can be any valid address, such as the loopback address (127.0.0.1), a specific network interface, or a wildcard address like 0.0.0.0 which means "bind to all available network interfaces." The port number should be unique and not in use by any other application on the machine.

Creating a TCP Listener with Tokio

By now, we already learned about Tokio in the previous chapter. We will straight away begin with creating a TCP listener with Tokio as below:

In your Rust code, import the necessary modules and set up the listener:

```
use tokio::net::TcpListener;

use tokio::io::{AsyncReadExt, AsyncWriteExt};


#[tokio::main]

async fn main() -> std::io::Result<()> {

    let listener =
TcpListener::bind("127.0.0.1:8080").await?;

    println!("Server listening on 127.0.0.1:8080");


    loop {

        let (mut socket, addr) =
listener.accept().await?;

        println!("New connection: {}", addr);


        tokio::spawn(async move {

            let mut buf = [0; 1024];

            loop {
```

```rust
        let n = match socket.read(&mut buf).await {
            Ok(n) if n == 0 => return,
            Ok(n) => n,
            Err(e) => {
                eprintln!("Failed to read from socket; err = {:?}", e);
                return;
            }
        };

        if let Err(e) = socket.write_all(&buf[0..n]).await {
            eprintln!("Failed to write to socket; err = {:?}", e);
            return;
        }
    }
});
    }
}
```

The above program binds the listener to 127.0.0.1:8080 and waits for incoming connections. For each new connection, it spawns a new task to handle the client, reading from and writing to the socket asynchronously.

Creating a TCP Listener with Mio

Mio (Metal IO) is a low-level, event-driven, non-blocking I/O library for Rust. It provides more control over I/O operations compared to high-level libraries like Tokio.

Add Mio as a Dependency

Add the following lines to your Cargo.toml file to include Mio:

```
[dependencies]

mio = "0.8"
```

Import Mio and Set Up the Listener

Import the necessary modules and create the TCP listener:

```
use mio::{Events, Interest, Poll, Token};

use mio::net::TcpListener;

use std::io;

use std::net::SocketAddr;


fn main() -> io::Result<()> {

    const SERVER: Token = Token(0);

    let address: SocketAddr =
"127.0.0.1:8080".parse().unwrap();

    let mut listener = TcpListener::bind(address)?;


    let mut poll = Poll::new()?;
```

```rust
    poll.registry().register(&mut listener, SERVER,
Interest::READABLE)?;


    let mut events = Events::with_capacity(128);


    loop {
        poll.poll(&mut events, None)?;


        for event in events.iter() {
            match event.token() {
                SERVER => {
                    let (mut socket, addr) =
listener.accept()?;

                    println!("New connection: {}", addr);


                    // Read and write to the socket
                    let mut buf = [0; 1024];
                    loop {
                        match socket.read(&mut buf) {
                            Ok(0) => break, // Connection
closed

                            Ok(n) =>
socket.write_all(&buf[0..n])?,
```

```rust
                    Err(e) => {
                        eprintln!("Error reading
socket: {:?}", e);
                        break;
                    }
                }
            }
        },
        _ => (),
    }
}
}
}
```

This code sets up a TCP listener on 127.0.0.1:8080, uses the Poll object to wait for events, and handles incoming connections by reading from and writing to the socket.

Creating a TCP Listener with Rust-Async

Rust-Async encompasses libraries like async-std that provide tools for writing asynchronous code. Given below is how to create a TCP listener using async-std:

Add async-std as a Dependency

Add the following lines to your Cargo.toml file:

```toml
[dependencies]

async-std = "1.10"
```

Import async-std and Create Listener

In your Rust code, set up the TCP listener:

```rust
use async_std::net::{TcpListener, TcpStream};

use async_std::prelude::*;


async fn handle_connection(mut stream: TcpStream) ->
std::io::Result<()> {

    let mut buf = [0; 1024];

    loop {

        let n = stream.read(&mut buf).await?;

        if n == 0 {

            break; // Connection closed

        }

        stream.write_all(&buf[0..n]).await?;

    }

    Ok(())

}


#[async_std::main]

async fn main() -> std::io::Result<()> {

    let listener =
TcpListener::bind("127.0.0.1:8080").await?;
```

```
    println!("Listening on {}", listener.local_addr()?);


    while let Ok((stream, _)) = listener.accept().await {

async_std::task::spawn(handle_connection(stream));

    }

    Ok(())

}
```

The above program sets up a TCP listener on 127.0.0.1:8080, accepts incoming connections, and spawns a new task to handle each connection using async-std.

Accept Incoming Connections

When a TCP listener is created, it starts listening for incoming connection requests on a specified IP address and port number. Once a connection request is received from a remote client, the listener accepts the request and returns a TCP stream. This TCP stream is then used to communicate with the remote client, allowing data to be sent and received over the network.

Following are the steps to accept connections:

- The first step involves binding to a specific IP address and port number to create a TCP listener. This listener is responsible for accepting incoming connection requests.

- Once the listener is created, it continuously listens for incoming connection requests from remote clients.

- Upon receiving a connection request, the listener accepts it and creates a new TCP stream to handle communication with the remote client.

- The newly created TCP stream is used to send and receive data between the local and remote hosts. This communication continues until the connection is closed by either party.

Accept Incoming Connections using Tokio

Following is the script to accept incoming connections using Tokio:

```rust
use std::net::SocketAddr;

use tokio::net::{TcpListener, TcpStream};


#[tokio::main]
async fn main() -> Result<(), Box<dyn std::error::Error>>
{
    let address: SocketAddr = "127.0.0.1:8080".parse()?;

    let listener = TcpListener::bind(&address).await?;


    loop {
        let (socket, _) = listener.accept().await?;

        tokio::spawn(async move {

            handle_client(socket).await;

        });
    }
    Ok(())

}


async fn handle_client(mut socket: TcpStream) ->
Result<(), Box<dyn std::error::Error>> {
    // handle the client connection here

    Ok(())
```

```
}
```

In the above script,

- The listener waits for incoming connections in an asynchronous loop. Upon accepting a connection, a new task is spawned to handle the client using tokio::spawn.

- The handle_client function then processes the client connection.

Accept Incoming Connections using Mio

Following is an example of accepting incoming connections using Mio:

```
use mio::{Events, Interest, Poll, Token};

use mio::net::{TcpListener, TcpStream};


const SERVER: Token = Token(0);


fn main() -> std::io::Result<()> {

    let address = "127.0.0.1:8080".parse().unwrap();

    let mut listener = TcpListener::bind(address)?;


    let poll = Poll::new()?;

    let mut events = Events::with_capacity(128);


    poll.registry().register(&mut listener, SERVER,
Interest::READABLE)?;
```

```
loop {

    poll.poll(&mut events, None)?;

    for event in events.iter() {
        match event.token() {
            SERVER => {
                let (mut stream, _) =
listener.accept()?;

                poll.registry().register(&mut stream,
Token(1), Interest::READABLE)?;
            },
            Token(1) => {
                let mut buf = [0; 1024];
                let mut stream =
TcpStream::from_std(event.into_tcp_stream().unwrap())?;

                stream.read(&mut buf)?;

                // handle incoming data
            },
            _ => (),
        }
    }
}
```

```
}
```

In the above script,

The listener is registered with a Poll instance to monitor readiness events. The poll object waits for events, and when an event occurs, it checks if it corresponds to the listener or a client connection. The new connections are accepted and registered with the poll instance, and data is read from the client streams.

Accept Incoming Connections using async-std

Let us look at an example to accept incoming connections using async-std:

```
use async_std::net::{TcpListener, TcpStream};

use async_std::task;


async fn handle_client(mut stream: TcpStream) {

    // handle incoming data

}


async fn listen_for_connections() -> std::io::Result<()>
{

    let address = "127.0.0.1:8080".parse().unwrap();

    let listener = TcpListener::bind(address).await?;


    loop {

        let (stream, _) = listener.accept().await?;

        task::spawn(handle_client(stream));
```

```
    }

}

fn main() -> std::io::Result<()> {

    task::block_on(listen_for_connections())

}
```

In the above, the listener accepts incoming connections in an asynchronous loop. And for each new connection, a new task is spawned using task::spawn to handle the client connection. Whether using Tokio, Mio, or async-std, the process generally involves creating a TCP listener, waiting for incoming connection requests, accepting these requests, and handling the resulting connections using TCP streams.

Processing of Incoming Data

Overview

When a client sends data to a TCP server, the data arrives as a stream of bytes. The server must interpret this byte stream to understand the client's message and respond accordingly. For instance, in a chat application, the server extracts the message text from the byte stream and may also need to validate the user or check the message's format before storing or broadcasting it.

Another example is a file server where the client requests a file download. The server needs to interpret the request, locate the file, and send it back to the client. This process involves correctly reading the incoming data, processing the request, and handling any errors.

Following are the key steps in processing incoming data as below:

- The server reads data from the TCP stream in chunks. This data is usually read into a buffer for further processing.

- The server interprets the byte stream to extract meaningful information, such as commands, messages, or requests.

- Based on the interpreted data, the server performs necessary actions, such as storing messages, fetching files, or executing commands.

- After processing the data, the server sends an appropriate response back to the client.

- Throughout the process, the server must handle errors, such as malformed data, connection issues, or unauthorized requests.

Processing Incoming Data with Tokio

Take a look at the following sample program wherein we utilize Tokio to process incoming data:

```rust
use tokio::io::{AsyncReadExt, AsyncWriteExt};

use tokio::net::TcpListener;


async fn handle_connection(mut stream:
tokio::net::TcpStream) -> std::io::Result<()> {

    let mut buffer = [0; 1024];


    loop {

        let bytes_read = stream.read(&mut buffer).await?;

        if bytes_read == 0 {

            return Ok(());

        }


        let message =
String::from_utf8_lossy(&buffer[0..bytes_read]);

        println!("Received message: {}", message);


        stream.write_all(&buffer[0..bytes_read]).await?;
```

```rust
    }
}


#[tokio::main]

async fn main() -> std::io::Result<()> {

    let address = "127.0.0.1:8080";

    let listener =
TcpListener::bind(address).await.unwrap();


    println!("Listening on: {}", address);


    loop {

        let (stream, _) = listener.accept().await?;

        tokio::spawn(async move {

            if let Err(e) =
handle_connection(stream).await {

                eprintln!("An error occurred while
processing connection: {}", e);

            }

        });

    }

}
```

In the above sample program, the server reads data from the TCP stream, prints the received message, and echoes it back to the client. If no data is read (indicating the client has disconnected), the loop exits. It handles each connection in a separate asynchronous task using tokio::spawn.

Processing Incoming Data with Mio

Have a look at the following example of a program that makes use of Mio to process data that is being received:

```
use mio::{Events, Poll, Token};

use mio::net::{TcpListener, TcpStream};

use std::collections::HashMap;

use std::net::SocketAddr;

use std::io::{Read, Write};



const SERVER: Token = Token(0);



struct Connection {

    socket: TcpStream,

    address: SocketAddr,

    buffer: Vec<u8>,

}



impl Connection {

    fn new(socket: TcpStream, address: SocketAddr) ->
Connection {
```

```rust
        Connection {
            socket,
            address,
            buffer: vec![0; 1024],
        }
    }


    fn readable(&mut self) -> std::io::Result<()> {
        let bytes_read = self.socket.read(&mut self.buffer)?;


        if bytes_read == 0 {
            println!("Client disconnected: {}", self.address);
        } else {
            let message = String::from_utf8_lossy(&self.buffer[0..bytes_read]);
            println!("Received message: {}", message);


            self.socket.write_all(&self.buffer[0..bytes_read])?;
        }
```

```rust
        Ok(())

    }

}


fn main() -> std::io::Result<()> {

    let address = "127.0.0.1:8080".parse().unwrap();

    let listener = TcpListener::bind(&address)?;

    let poll = Poll::new()?;

    let mut events = Events::with_capacity(1024);

    let mut connections = HashMap::new();


    poll.registry().register(&listener, SERVER,
mio::Interest::READABLE)?;


    loop {

        poll.poll(&mut events, None)?;


        for event in events.iter() {

            match event.token() {

                SERVER => {

                    let (socket, address) =
listener.accept()?;
```

```rust
                        println!("Accepted connection from: {}", address);

                        let connection =
Connection::new(socket, address);

                        let token = Token(connections.len() +
1);

poll.registry().register(&connection.socket, token,
mio::Interest::READABLE)?;

                        connections.insert(token,
connection);
                    },
                    token => {
                        let mut connection =
connections.get_mut(&token).unwrap();
                        if event.is_readable() {
                            connection.readable()?;
                        }
                    }
                }
            }
        }
    }
}
```

In this Mio sample program, the server uses a Poll instance to monitor events. Each connection is stored in a Connection struct, which handles reading and writing data. The server registers the listener and each connection with the poll instance, processing data when events occur.

Processing Incoming Data with async-std

For an example of how we use async-std to process incoming data, take a look at the following sample program:

```
use async_std::net::{TcpListener, TcpStream};

use async_std::task;

use async_std::prelude::*;


async fn handle_connection(mut stream: TcpStream) ->
std::io::Result<()> {

    let mut buffer = [0; 1024];


    loop {

        let bytes_read = stream.read(&mut buffer).await?;


        if bytes_read == 0 {

            return Ok(());

        }


        let message =
String::from_utf8_lossy(&buffer[0..bytes_read]);

        println!("Received message: {}", message);
```

```rust
        stream.write_all(&buffer[0..bytes_read]).await?;

    }

}


#[async_std::main]

async fn main() -> std::io::Result<()> {

    let listener =
TcpListener::bind("127.0.0.1:8080").await?;

    println!("Listening on {}", listener.local_addr()?);


    while let Ok((stream, addr)) =
listener.accept().await {

        println!("Accepted connection from {}", addr);


        task::spawn(handle_connection(stream));

    }


    Ok(())

}
```

In the above async-std sample program, each connection is handled by spawning a new task using task::spawn, which processes the incoming data and echoes it back to the client. To summarize, using libraries like Tokio, Mio, and async-std offers different levels of abstraction and control, allowing developers to choose the right tool for their specific network demands.

Managing Errors

When developing reliable network applications, error management is an important consideration, especially for TCP/IP applications. Better user experiences and continued security are the results of applications that have proper error handling and can gracefully handle unexpected issues. Following are some of the prime reasons why error handling is of utmost importance for any networking application:

- Unhandled errors can cause applications to crash or behave unpredictably. Handling errors helps applications recover gracefully and continue operating.

- Clear error messages help users understand issues and potential resolutions, reducing frustration.

- Proper error handling can mitigate risks of denial-of-service attacks, data breaches, and other security vulnerabilities by preventing unintentional exposure of sensitive information.

Handling Errors using Tokio

In Tokio, the Result type is extensively used to handle errors. This type represents either a successful value (Ok) or an error (Err). Many Tokio functions return a Result, allowing errors to be propagated up the call stack using the ? operator.

Given below is a quick example:

```
use tokio::io::{AsyncReadExt, AsyncWriteExt};

use tokio::net::{TcpListener, TcpStream};



async fn process_connection(mut stream: TcpStream) ->
Result<(), Box<dyn std::error::Error>> {

    let mut buf = [0; 1024];

    loop {

        let n = stream.read(&mut buf).await?;
```

```rust
        if n == 0 {
            // End of stream
            return Ok(());
        }

        println!("Received {} bytes: {:?}", n,
&buf[0..n]);

        stream.write_all(&buf[0..n]).await?;
    }
}


#[tokio::main]
async fn main() -> Result<(), Box<dyn std::error::Error>>
{
    let listener =
TcpListener::bind("127.0.0.1:8080").await?;

    println!("Listening on {}", listener.local_addr()?);


    loop {
        let (stream, addr) = listener.accept().await?;
        println!("Accepted connection from {}", addr);


        tokio::spawn(async move {
```

```
            if let Err(e) =
process_connection(stream).await {
                eprintln!("Error: {}", e);
            }
        });
    }
    Ok(())
}
```

In the above given example,

- The process_connection function reads from and writes to the TCP stream. If any read or write operation fails, the ? operator propagates the error.

- In the main function, errors from process_connection are handled using if let Err(e) = process_connection(stream).await, printing error messages to standard error.

Handling Errors using Mio

Mio, a low-level library for non-blocking I/O, also uses the Result type for error handling. The io::Result type, which is a specialized version of Result, is often used.

Given below is a quick example:

```
use mio::net::{TcpListener, TcpStream};

use mio::{Events, Poll, Token};

use std::collections::HashMap;

use std::error::Error;

use std::io::{Read, Write};


const SERVER: Token = Token(0);
```

```rust
struct Connection {

    stream: TcpStream,

    buf: Vec<u8>,

}


fn main() -> Result<(), Box<dyn Error>> {

    let addr = "127.0.0.1:8080".parse()?;

    let listener = TcpListener::bind(addr)?;

    let mut poll = Poll::new()?;

    let mut events = Events::with_capacity(128);

    let mut connections = HashMap::new();


    poll.registry().register(&listener, SERVER,
mio::Interest::READABLE)?;


    loop {
        poll.poll(&mut events, None)?;
        for event in events.iter() {
            match event.token() {
                SERVER => {
```

```rust
                    let (stream, addr) =
listener.accept()?;

                    let conn = Connection {
                        stream,
                        buf: vec![0; 1024],
                    };

                    let token = Token(connections.len() +
1);

poll.registry().register(&conn.stream, token,
mio::Interest::READABLE)?;

                    connections.insert(token, conn);
                    println!("Accepted connection from
{}", addr);

                }
                token => {
                    let done = if let Some(conn) =
connections.get_mut(&token) {

                        match conn.stream.read(&mut
conn.buf) {

                            Ok(0) => true,

                            Ok(n) => {

                                println!("Received {}
bytes: {:?}", n, &conn.buf[..n]);
```

```
conn.stream.write_all(&conn.buf[..n])?;
                                false
                            }
                        Err(e) => {
                            eprintln!("Error reading
from socket: {}", e);
                            true
                        }
                    }
                } else {
                    false
                };
                if done {
                    connections.remove(&token);
                }
            }
        }
    }
}
```

In the above sample program, the connection struct manages the TCP stream and buffer. The main function sets up a Poll instance to handle multiple connections, registering each connection and handling read/write operations. And, errors during read/write operations are logged using eprintln!.

Handling Errors using async-std

Async-std provides a high-level, ergonomic API for asynchronous I/O, similar to Tokio, with built-in support for error handling via the Result type.

Given below is a quick example:

```
use async_std::net::{TcpListener, TcpStream};

use async_std::task;

use async_std::prelude::*;


async fn handle_connection(mut stream: TcpStream) ->
std::io::Result<()> {

    let mut buffer = [0; 1024];


    loop {

        let bytes_read = stream.read(&mut buffer).await?;


        if bytes_read == 0 {

            return Ok(());

        }


        let message =
String::from_utf8_lossy(&buffer[0..bytes_read]);
```

```rust
        println!("Received message: {}", message);


        stream.write_all(&buffer[0..bytes_read]).await?;

    }

}


#[async_std::main]

async fn main() -> std::io::Result<()> {

    let listener =
TcpListener::bind("127.0.0.1:8080").await?;

    println!("Listening on {}", listener.local_addr()?);


    while let Ok((stream, addr)) =
listener.accept().await {

        println!("Accepted connection from {}", addr);


        task::spawn(async move {

            if let Err(e) =
handle_connection(stream).await {

                eprintln!("Error: {}", e);

            }

        });
```

```
    }


    Ok(())
}
```

In the above given example,

- The handle_connection function processes incoming data and echoes it back to the client. The errors are propagated using the ? operator.

- The main function listens for connections and spawns tasks to handle them and the errors are logged using eprintln!.

When working with libraries such as Tokio, Mio, and async-std in an asynchronous environment, a simple and effective way to handle errors is by utilizing Rust's Result type and the? operator.

Summary

Just to summarize, we explored the intricacies of managing TCP/IP connections using Rust. We learned about the importance of port selection in avoiding conflicts with other applications and ensuring smooth communication. The chapter emphasized the critical role of binding sockets to specific IP addresses and port numbers, allowing applications to listen for incoming connections. We delved into the process of accepting incoming connections, where a listener establishes a TCP connection with a remote client, creating a stream for data communication.

The topic on processing incoming data highlighted how servers receive and handle data streams from clients, extracting relevant information and responding appropriately. This involved not only reading and interpreting the data but also managing potential errors that could arise during communication. By learning the error handling mechanisms in detail, we understood how to maintain robustness, enhance user experience, and ensure security. The practical examples provided using the Tokio, Mio, and async-std libraries illustrated different approaches to managing TCP connections and handling errors. These examples demonstrated the use of Rust's Result type and the ? operator to propagate errors and maintain clean, readable code.

Overall, this chapter equipped us with a comprehensive understanding of setting up and managing TCP/IP connections, focusing on the practical aspects of port selection, binding sockets, accepting connections, processing data, and handling errors to build reliable and secure network applications.

CHAPTER 8: PACKET & NETWORK ANALYSIS

Understanding Packets

What are Packets?

In computer networking, data is transmitted across a network in small units called packets. These packets are essential for carrying information between devices on the network, including the actual data, headers, and control information necessary for proper communication.

A packet is typically composed of two main parts: a header and a payload. The header contains metadata about the packet, such as the source and destination IP addresses, the protocol in use, and various flags or control information that help manage the packet's journey across the network. The payload contains the actual data being transmitted, such as the contents of an email, a file, or any other type of data. When a device sends data over a network, the data is divided into packets, each of which is transmitted separately and can take different paths to reach the destination. The receiving device then reassembles these packets to reconstruct the original data.

Understanding Packet Analysis

Packet analysis is the process of examining the headers and payloads of packets to understand network traffic. This can be done manually by using network analyzers or packet sniffers, or programmatically by analyzing packets with software tools.

Packet analysis serves several purposes:

- Identifying bottlenecks or performance issues within the network. For instance, by examining packet delays or loss, administrators can pinpoint problematic network segments.

- Monitoring and optimizing network performance by analyzing the traffic patterns and loads. This can help in planning for capacity upgrades or detecting inefficient routes.

- Detecting potential security threats such as unauthorized access, malware, or intrusion attempts. By inspecting packet contents and patterns, security analysts can identify and mitigate threats.

- Investigating network incidents by analyzing packet data to understand what happened during a security breach or network failure. This involves tracing the path of packets and examining their contents for clues.

A fundamental aspect of packet analysis is examining the source and destination addresses. This information helps understand the flow of traffic across the network and can reveal unusual or suspicious patterns, such as an unexpected spike in traffic from a particular source. Additionally, the protocol used in the packet, such as TCP, UDP, or HTTP, provides context about the type of communication and its expected behavior.

The payload of a packet can also offer valuable insights. For instance, inspecting HTTP request and response contents can provide information about web application behavior and potential vulnerabilities. Similarly, analyzing email contents can reveal spam or phishing attempts.

Packet Analysis Tools Overview

Tools for packet analysis include network analyzers like Wireshark, which allow detailed inspection of packet contents, and various libraries in programming languages like Rust that facilitate programmatic packet analysis. These tools can capture real-time network traffic and provide a granular view of the data being transmitted, helping administrators and security analysts perform their tasks more effectively.

Libraries like pcap and libpnet can be used for packet capture and analysis. These libraries provide APIs to capture packets from the network interface, filter them based on various criteria, and analyze their contents programmatically. While doing packet analysis, it is important to keep in mind that the network's efficiency and security are also key considerations. By delving into packet headers and payloads, security analysts and network administrators can understand how networks behave, spot problems or threats, and fix them or prevent them.

Packet Manipulation Tools

Packet manipulation libraries provide a variety of functionalities, including packet creation, modification, capture, analysis, and protocol parsing. These capabilities are essential for network engineers to perform tasks like building custom packets, modifying existing traffic, capturing real-time network data, and understanding protocol behavior.

Following are the capabilities of packet manipulation tools in detail:

- Packet Creation - Packet manipulation libraries allow developers to create custom packets from scratch. This involves specifying values for all packet fields, including headers, payloads, and control information. Custom packet creation is beneficial for building network applications, testing devices, and generating traffic for analysis.

- Packet Modification - Developers can use these libraries to modify existing packets, adjusting values of packet fields or adding/removing headers and payloads. This functionality is valuable for testing, analyzing traffic, and implementing security measures like packet filtering and traffic shaping.

- Packet Capture and Analysis - Many packet manipulation libraries offer functions to capture packets from network interfaces and analyze them in real-time. This capability is essential for troubleshooting network issues, monitoring performance, and identifying security threats.

- Protocol Parsing - These libraries often include tools for parsing and interpreting various network protocols such as TCP/IP, HTTP, and DNS. Protocol parsing enables developers to work with network data at a higher abstraction level, facilitating detailed analysis and troubleshooting.

For our learning, we will select two popular packet manipulation libraries, one is pnet and the other one is libtins. We will learn them in detail in the upcoming section.

pnet

The pnet library is a popular choice for packet manipulation, offering a comprehensive set of functions and data structures for creating, modifying, and analyzing network packets. It is designed to be cross-platform, supporting multiple operating systems and a wide range of protocols.

Following are the key attributes of pnet:

- pnet supports various network protocols, including TCP, UDP, ICMP, IP, and Ethernet. This extensive protocol support allows network engineers to work with different types of network traffic.

- pnet works on Windows, macOS, and Linux, making it versatile for use across different environments.

- With pnet, developers can create custom packets by specifying values for all packet fields. This feature is useful for testing network devices, generating test traffic, and building network applications.

- pnet enables developers to modify existing packets, which is essential for testing and implementing security measures.

- pnet provides functions to capture and analyze packets in real-time, aiding in network troubleshooting, performance analysis, and security monitoring.

Given below is a sample code snippet demonstrating how to create and send a custom TCP packet using pnet:

```
use pnet::packet::tcp::{MutableTcpPacket, TcpFlags};

use pnet::packet::Packet;

use pnet::transport::{transport_channel,
TransportChannelType, TransportProtocol};


// Create a new TCP packet
```

```
let mut tcp_packet =
MutableTcpPacket::new(tcp_buffer).unwrap();

tcp_packet.set_source(1234);

tcp_packet.set_destination(80);

tcp_packet.set_flags(TcpFlags::SYN);


// Create a transport channel and send the packet

let (mut tcp_sender, _) = transport_channel(4096,
TransportChannelType::Layer4(TransportProtocol::Tcp)).unw
rap();

tcp_sender.send_to(tcp_packet, IpAddr::V4(ipv4_addr));
```

libtins

The libtins library is another powerful Rust library for capturing and analyzing network traffic. It offers a high-level API for working with network packets and includes tools for traffic analysis, packet filtering, and protocol decoding.

Following are the key features of libtins:

- libtins provides a high-level API for capturing network traffic, supporting live, offline, and remote capture modes. It can capture traffic from various interfaces and protocols.

- libtins includes tools for filtering, decoding, and analyzing packets. It supports a wide range of protocols and allows for detailed packet analysis.

- Developers can create and send custom packets with libtins, specifying all necessary packet fields. This feature is beneficial for testing, traffic generation, and application development.

- libtins works on multiple operating systems, making it suitable for use in diverse environments.

Given below is a sample code snippet demonstrating how to capture network traffic using libtins:

```
use libtins::{Config, Interface};
```

```
// Create a new configuration object

let config = Config::default();


// Open a network interface for capturing traffic

let iface = Interface::new("eth0").unwrap();


// Start the capture loop and process incoming packets

let mut capture = iface.capture(&config).unwrap();

while let Some(packet) = capture.next() {

    println!("Received packet: {:?}", packet);

}
```

Both of these above discussed libraries enable the creation, modification, capture, and analysis of network packets, facilitating network troubleshooting, performance monitoring, and security analysis.

Create a Packet Capture Loop

A packet capture loop is a programming construct used to capture and process network packets in real-time. It involves setting up a loop that continuously listens for incoming packets on a network interface, and then processes each packet as it arrives.

Process Overview

The process of creating a packet capture loop typically involves the following steps:

- The first step in creating a packet capture loop is to open a network interface that will be used for capturing packets. This is usually done using a platform-specific API or library, such as libpcap on Unix-like systems or WinPcap on Windows.

- Once the network interface is open, it is necessary to configure the capture parameters, such as the maximum size of the captured packets or the type of traffic to capture. This is usually done using a set of configuration options that can be passed to the capture API or library.

- With the network interface and capture configuration set up, it is now possible to start the packet capture loop. This involves setting up a loop that listens for incoming packets on the network interface, and then processes each packet as it arrives.

- As packets are received by the capture loop, they are typically passed to a packet processing function that extracts relevant information from the packet and performs any necessary actions. This might involve decoding the packet headers, analyzing the packet payload, or even modifying the packet and sending it back out on the network.

- Once the capture is complete, it is necessary to stop the packet capture loop and close the network interface.

Capturing Packets using pnet

Following is an example of how to create a packet capture loop using pnet:

```rust
use pnet::datalink::{self, NetworkInterface};

use pnet::packet::{Packet, tcp::TcpPacket};

use pnet::packet::ethernet::EthernetPacket;

use pnet::packet::ip::IpNextHeaderProtocols;

use pnet::packet::ipv4::Ipv4Packet;

use pnet::packet::udp::UdpPacket;


fn main() {

    // Get a list of available network interfaces

    let interfaces = datalink::interfaces();


    // Select the first interface
```

```rust
    let interface = &interfaces[0];


    // Create a packet capture channel on the interface

    let (_, mut rx) = match datalink::channel(&interface,
Default::default()) {

        Ok((_, rx)) => rx,

        Err(e) => panic!("Failed to create packet capture
channel: {}", e),

    };


    // Create a buffer to hold incoming packets

    let mut buffer = [0u8; 65536];


    loop {

        // Receive the next packet from the channel

        match rx.next() {

            Ok(packet) => {

                // Parse the packet as an Ethernet packet

                let ethernet_packet =
EthernetPacket::new(packet).unwrap();


                // If the packet is an IP packet, parse
it as such
```

```rust
            if ethernet_packet.get_ethertype() ==
0x0800 {

                let ipv4_packet =
Ipv4Packet::new(ethernet_packet.payload()).unwrap();


                // If the packet is a TCP packet,
parse it as such

                if
ipv4_packet.get_next_level_protocol() ==
IpNextHeaderProtocols::Tcp {

                    let tcp_packet =
TcpPacket::new(ipv4_packet.payload()).unwrap();


                    // Print the source and
destination IP addresses and port numbers
                    println!("{}:{} -> {}:{}",

                        ipv4_packet.get_source(),

                        tcp_packet.get_source(),

ipv4_packet.get_destination(),

tcp_packet.get_destination());
                }
```

```rust
                // If the packet is a UDP packet,
parse it as such

                if
ipv4_packet.get_next_level_protocol() ==
IpNextHeaderProtocols::Udp {

                    let udp_packet =
UdpPacket::new(ipv4_packet.payload()).unwrap();


                    // Print the source and
destination IP addresses and port numbers
                    println!("{}:{} -> {}:{}",

                        ipv4_packet.get_source(),

                        udp_packet.get_source(),

ipv4_packet.get_destination(),

udp_packet.get_destination());

                }
            }
        },

        Err(e) => panic!("Failed to receive packet:
{}", e),

    }

}
```

```
}
```

In the above sample program, we start by getting a list of available network interfaces using datalink::interfaces() from the pnet library. We then select the first interface and create a packet capture channel on it using datalink::channel(). This function returns a tuple of a transmitter and a receiver, which we store in tx and rx variables, respectively.

Next, we set up a loop that listens for incoming packets using the rx.next() method. This method returns a Result object that contains a Packet object if a packet is received successfully. We use EthernetPacket::new() to parse the received packet as an Ethernet packet.

If the received packet is an IP packet, we use Ipv4Packet::new() to parse it as an IPv4 packet. We further parse the IPv4 packet as a TCP or UDP packet using TcpPacket::new() or UdpPacket::new(), respectively. We then print the source and destination IP addresses and port numbers.

Process the Captured Packets

Overview

Processing captured packets involves analyzing and manipulating network packets that have been intercepted using tools like Wireshark or tcpdump. This process is crucial for diagnosing network problems, optimizing performance, and identifying security issues.

When processing captured packets, you need to examine both the headers and the payloads of the packets. Headers provide information about the source and destination IP addresses, port numbers, and other protocol-specific data. The payload contains the actual data being transmitted.

Below is a quick procedure to process captured packets:

- The initial step is to examine the various headers present in the packet, such as the Ethernet header, IP header, and transport protocol header (TCP or UDP). This helps in understanding the basic details of the packet like source and destination IP addresses, port numbers, and the protocol used.

- After analyzing the headers, focus on the payload, which contains the actual data being transmitted. This can include application-specific headers or metadata.

- Based on the analysis, you can filter packets according to specific criteria such as IP address, port number, or protocol type. You can also manipulate the packets by altering their data or headers.

Processing Captured Packets using pnet

First, set up packet capture using the Capture struct provided by pnet:

```rust
use pnet::datalink::{self, NetworkInterface,
Channel::Ethernet};

use pnet::packet::{Packet, ethernet::EthernetPacket,
ip::IpNextHeaderProtocols, ipv4::Ipv4Packet,
tcp::TcpPacket, udp::UdpPacket};


fn capture_packets(interface: NetworkInterface) {

    let (_, mut rx) = match datalink::channel(&interface,
Default::default()) {

        Ok(Ethernet(_, rx)) => rx,

        Ok(_) => panic!("Unhandled channel type"),

        Err(e) => panic!("Failed to create datalink
channel: {}", e),

    };


    let mut iter = rx.iter();

    while let Some(packet) = iter.next() {

        let ethernet =
EthernetPacket::new(packet).unwrap();

        match ethernet.get_ethertype() {

            pnet::packet::ethernet::EtherTypes::Ipv4 => {

                let ipv4 =
Ipv4Packet::new(ethernet.payload()).unwrap();
```

```rust
                    match ipv4.get_next_level_protocol() {
                        IpNextHeaderProtocols::Tcp => {
                            let tcp =
TcpPacket::new(ipv4.payload()).unwrap();
                                process_tcp_packet(&tcp);
                        }
                        IpNextHeaderProtocols::Udp => {
                            let udp =
UdpPacket::new(ipv4.payload()).unwrap();
                                process_udp_packet(&udp);
                        }
                        _ => {}
                    }
                }
                _ => {}
            }
        }
    }
}

fn process_tcp_packet(packet: &TcpPacket) {
    println!("TCP Packet: {} -> {}",
        packet.get_source(),
```

```rust
        packet.get_destination());

    // Add further TCP processing logic here
}


fn process_udp_packet(packet: &UdpPacket) {
    println!("UDP Packet: {} -> {}",
        packet.get_source(),
        packet.get_destination());
    // Add further UDP processing logic here
}


fn main() {
    let interfaces = datalink::interfaces();

    let interface = interfaces.into_iter()
        .filter(|iface| iface.is_up() &&
!iface.is_loopback() && iface.ips.iter().any(|ip|
ip.is_ipv4()))
        .next()
        .expect("No suitable network interface found");


    capture_packets(interface);
}
```

In the above sample program,

- The code begins by retrieving available network interfaces using datalink::interfaces(). It selects a suitable interface for capturing packets. The selected interface is used to create a packet capture channel. The datalink::channel function initializes the channel. The loop continuously listens for incoming packets. The rx.iter() method iterates over the captured packets.

- For each packet, the Ethernet header is parsed to check if it's an IPv4 packet. If it is, the IPv4 header is parsed further to check if it's a TCP or UDP packet. Depending on the protocol, the packet is passed to the appropriate processing function (process_tcp_packet or process_udp_packet).

Analyze Captured Packets

Overview

After processing captured packets, the next step is to analyze the data within them to gain insights into network traffic and detect security threats or anomalies. Packet analysis involves examining the content of individual packets and the relationships between packets to identify patterns and trends that reveal useful information about the network. This can include examining the headers and payloads of packets and the timing and frequency of packet transmissions.

In fact, packet analysis is essential across various applications:

- network engineers can identify network bottlenecks, packet loss, and other issues causing slow performance or other problems.

- Security analysts can detect and respond to various types of attacks, including malware, phishing, and other forms of cybercrime, by analyzing network traffic. Packet analysis helps identify the source and nature of attacks and the extent of any damage.

- Network administrators can better understand how their networks are used and can accordingly optimize performance.

Sample Program: Analyzing Packets

Let us learn and practice to perform and experience the process of packet analysis. We will continue using the pnet library.

Capturing Packets

First, use the pnet_packet_capture library to capture packets from a network interface. Below is an example code snippet that captures 100 packets from the eth0 interface:

```rust
use pnet_packet_capture::{PacketCapture, Packet};


fn capture_packets() {

    let mut cap =
PacketCapture::from_device("eth0").unwrap();

    cap.open().unwrap();

    let mut count = 0;

    while let Some(packet) = cap.next() {

        count += 1;

        if count >= 100 {

            break;

        }

        analyze_packet(packet.data);

    }

}
```

In the above sample program, the capture_packets function initializes a packet capture on the eth0 interface and captures 100 packets. Each captured packet is passed to the analyze_packet function for further analysis.

Analyzing Captured Packets

Next, define a function to analyze each captured packet. In the below example, the function prints the source and destination IP addresses of each IPv4 packet:

```rust
use pnet::packet::Packet;
```

```
fn analyze_packet(packet: &[u8]) {

    let ipv4_packet =
pnet::packet::ipv4::Ipv4Packet::new(packet);

    if let Some(ipv4_packet) = ipv4_packet {

        let src = ipv4_packet.get_source();

        let dst = ipv4_packet.get_destination();

        println!("Source IP: {}, Destination IP: {}",
src, dst);

    }

}
```

The analyze_packet function checks if the packet is an IPv4 packet and, if so, prints the source and destination IP addresses.

Running Packet Capture and Analysis

Finally, call the capture_packets function to capture and analyze packets from the eth0 interface:

```
fn main() {

    capture_packets();

}
```

After this, there are many other things you can do with packet analysis such as:

- Extract and analyze the data portion of packets to understand the content being transmitted.

- Decode protocols like HTTP, DNS, and others to gain deeper insights into the nature of the network traffic.

- Implement algorithms to detect unusual patterns or behaviors that might indicate performance issues or security threats.

Summary

In this chapter, we covered a wide range of topics related to network security and packet analysis. We started by learning the importance of network security and the types of security measures that can be implemented in enterprise networks. We then moved on to packet analysis and what it means to capture, process, and analyze packets in a network.

We explored two popular Rust libraries, pnet and libtin, that can be used for packet manipulation and analysis. We learned the syntax and benefits of each library, and how they can be used by networking engineers to analyze network traffic and detect potential security threats. To demonstrate how to use pnet for packet capture and analysis, we walked through several practical examples of Rust code. We covered how to create a packet capture loop, process captured packets, and analyze them for useful information like source and destination IP addresses.

In summary, this chapter covered a lot of ground on the topics of network security and packet analysis. We explored several libraries and code snippets that can be used to capture, process, and analyze network traffic, and we learned the importance of these tools for detecting and preventing potential security threats in enterprise networks.

CHAPTER 9: NETWORK PERFORMANCE MONITORING

Network Performance Monitoring Overview

Monitoring a network involves systematically collecting and analyzing data related to the performance and status of a computer network. This data encompasses traffic flow, device activity, bandwidth usage, network health, and other relevant metrics. Through network monitoring, professionals can gain valuable insights into the functioning of the network and identify potential issues or areas for improvement. One of the primary benefits of network monitoring is the enhancement of network performance. By analyzing traffic and other key metrics, professionals can pinpoint slowdowns or bottlenecks within the network, enabling them to take steps to optimize and improve overall performance. Monitoring also allows for proactive issue identification; by spotting unusual behavior or high levels of activity in specific devices, administrators can address issues before they escalate into significant disruptions.

Network monitoring is crucial for enhancing security as well. By closely observing network activity, administrators can detect suspicious behavior or unusual traffic patterns that might indicate a security breach. Promptly addressing these issues helps prevent unauthorized access and other security threats. Moreover, monitoring can lead to substantial cost savings. By identifying over-utilized or under-utilized areas of the network, administrators can optimize resources and reduce unnecessary expenses. They can also determine which hardware or software is outdated or inefficient and recommend upgrades or replacements accordingly. Compliance with regulatory standards is another benefit of network monitoring, as many industries require specific monitoring practices to avoid costly fines or penalties.

Several tools and techniques are available to network professionals for monitoring network activity and performance. Network monitoring software provides real-time data on traffic, device activity, and other metrics, allowing for customized monitoring solutions tailored to organizational needs. Analyzing network traffic through techniques such as packet capture, flow analysis, and deep packet inspection can reveal patterns and trends, offering insights into network behavior and potential issues. Log analysis is another valuable technique, as log files generated by network devices and servers contain information on device activity, resource utilization, and security events, aiding in the overall analysis of network performance and security.

Performance monitoring involves tracking key metrics such as CPU usage, memory usage, and disk space usage for network devices and servers. Monitoring these metrics helps identify potential issues before they become major problems. Security monitoring focuses on detecting potential threats by scrutinizing network activity for unusual traffic patterns, unauthorized access attempts, and suspicious activity in logs. Combining these techniques provides a comprehensive approach to network monitoring, ensuring that all aspects of network performance and security are covered.

Effective network monitoring integrates seamlessly with existing network infrastructure and management systems, facilitating streamlined data collection and analysis. Automation plays a critical role in modern network monitoring, as automated systems can continuously monitor network activity and generate alerts when anomalies are detected. These alerts enable swift responses to potential issues, minimizing downtime and maintaining network performance.

Regular audits and reviews of network performance and security are essential for proactive network management and continuous improvement. By periodically reviewing network data, administrators can identify trends and recurring issues, allowing them to make informed decisions and implement necessary changes.

Metrics & Indicators

Understanding Network Performance Metrics

Bandwidth Usage

Network performance metrics are crucial for IT companies to track and analyze to ensure optimal network performance. One of the most critical metrics is bandwidth usage, which refers to the amount of data being transmitted over a network at any given time. Monitoring bandwidth usage helps identify potential bottlenecks or congestion that may cause slow performance or downtime. Another essential metric is latency, which measures the time it takes for a data packet to travel from one point on the network to another. High latency can lead to significant delays in network traffic, negatively impacting user experience and productivity.

Packet Loss

Packet loss, which refers to the number of data packets lost or dropped during transmission, is another important metric. High packet loss can indicate network congestion or other issues causing poor network performance. Network utilization, the percentage of available network resources currently used, needs to be monitored to ensure the network is not overburdened and to identify optimization opportunities. Error rates, which count errors or anomalies such as dropped packets, failed connections, or data corruption, also provide insight into network issues that need addressing to maintain optimal performance.

Network Availability

Network availability, the percentage of time the network is operational, is critical for ensuring users can access network resources when needed. Application response time, the time it takes for an application to respond to a user request, is crucial for ensuring applications perform optimally, allowing users to work efficiently. Device health, which refers to the status of individual network devices like routers, switches, and servers, must be monitored to ensure devices function properly and identify potential issues before they cause disruptions. Lastly, user experience, the quality of experience users have while using the network, should be monitored to ensure efficiency and effectiveness and identify areas for improvement.

Exploring Network Performance Indicators

Network performance indicators measure various aspects of network performance, including availability, utilization, and quality. Availability indicators, such as network uptime and application availability, measure the uptime of the network and its resources. Network uptime is the percentage of time the network is available and operational, serving as a key performance indicator (KPI) for ensuring network functionality and identifying improvement areas. Application availability measures the availability of individual applications within the network, ensuring users can access the necessary applications.

Availability Indicators

The benefits of monitoring availability indicators include reduced downtime and improved user experience. By identifying potential issues before they cause downtime, IT professionals can prevent lost productivity and revenue. When the network and its resources function properly, users can work more efficiently and effectively.

Utilization Indicators

Utilization indicators measure the percentage of network resources used at any given time. Bandwidth usage, which measures the amount of data transmitted over the network, helps IT professionals ensure the network is not overburdened and identify optimization areas. Network device utilization measures the percentage of available resources used by individual network devices, such as routers and switches, helping identify optimization opportunities and ensuring network efficiency.

Monitoring utilization indicators can improve network performance by identifying and addressing potential bottlenecks or congestion. It can also result in cost savings by optimizing network utilization, reducing the need for additional resources.

Quality Indicators

Quality indicators measure the quality of the network and its resources. Latency, which measures the time it takes for data to travel from one point to another, serves as a KPI for ensuring network efficiency and identifying improvement areas. Packet loss, which measures the number of data packets lost or dropped during transmission, helps identify potential network congestion or other issues causing poor performance.

Monitoring quality indicators improves user experience by ensuring the network operates efficiently without issues like latency and packet loss, allowing users to work more effectively. It also reduces the risk of data loss by identifying and addressing potential issues causing data loss.

Monitoring Network Availability

Network availability can be checked using the ping command and we can execute the ping command and capture its output using the std::process::Command struct.

Below is an implementation that demonstrates this process:

```rust
use std::process::Command;


fn check_network_availability(ip_address: &str) -> bool {

    let output = Command::new("ping")

        .arg("-c")

        .arg("1")

        .arg(ip_address)

        .output()

        .expect("Failed to execute command");


    output.status.success()

}
```

In this implementation, the check_network_availability function takes the IP address of the network device as a parameter. The Command struct is used to execute the ping command with the -c 1 option, which sends a single ICMP echo request packet to the specified IP address. The output of the command is captured, and the function returns true if the command executed successfully, indicating that the network device is available. If the command fails, the function returns false.

To send desktop notifications when the network device becomes unavailable, we use the notify-rust library. First, we add it to our Cargo.toml file:

```toml
[dependencies]

notify-rust = "4.0"
```

We can then use the following code to send a notification when the network device becomes unavailable:

```rust
use notify_rust::Notification;


fn send_notification() {

    Notification::new()

        .summary("Network device is unavailable")

        .body("The network device is not responding to pings")

        .show()

        .unwrap();

}
```

In this code, the send_notification function creates a new desktop notification using the Notification::new method. The summary and body of the notification are set using the summary and body methods, respectively. Finally, the show method displays the notification.

Next, we combine the previous implementations into a main function that periodically checks the availability of a network device and sends a notification if it becomes unavailable.

Below is how we do it:

```rust
use std::{thread, time};

use notify_rust::Notification;

use std::process::Command;


fn check_network_availability(ip_address: &str) -> bool {

    let output = Command::new("ping")

        .arg("-c")
```

```rust
        .arg("1")

        .arg(ip_address)

        .output()

        .expect("Failed to execute command");


    output.status.success()

}


fn send_notification() {

    Notification::new()

        .summary("Network device is unavailable")

        .body("The network device is not responding to
pings")

        .show()

        .unwrap();

}


fn main() {

    let ip_address = "192.168.0.1";

    let ping_interval = time::Duration::from_secs(10);


    loop {
```

```rust
        let is_available =
check_network_availability(ip_address);

        if !is_available {

            send_notification();

        }


        thread::sleep(ping_interval);

    }

}
```

After running this program, the IP address of the network device to monitor is set to "192.168.0.1". The ping interval is set to 10 seconds using the time::Duration::from_secs(10) method. The main function enters an infinite loop that periodically checks the availability of the network device using the check_network_availability function. The application will continuously check the availability of the network device specified by the IP address and send a desktop notification if the device becomes unavailable.

Monitoring Network Utilization

To monitor network utilization, we can use the get_if_addrs function from the ifaddrs crate and the sysctlbyname function from the libc crate. The get_if_addrs function retrieves a list of network interfaces and their associated IP addresses, while sysctlbyname retrieves network statistics for a specific interface. We can periodically retrieve network utilization statistics and calculate the network utilization percentage. Below is an easy implementation:

```rust
use ifaddrs::{get_if_addrs, IfAddr};

use libc::{c_ulong, if_data, ifmib};


fn get_network_utilization(interface_name: &str) ->
Option<f32> {
```

```rust
    let if_addrs = get_if_addrs().ok()?;

    let interface = if_addrs.iter().find(|ifaddr|
ifaddr.name == interface_name)?;


    let mut mib: ifmib = unsafe { std::mem::zeroed() };

    unsafe { libc::if_name2index(interface_name.as_ptr()
as *const i8) };


    let mut if_data: if_data = unsafe {
std::mem::zeroed() };

    let mut if_data_size = std::mem::size_of::<if_data>()
as c_ulong;


    if unsafe { libc::sysctlbyname(b"net.ifdata", &mut
if_data, &mut if_data_size, &mut mib, 5) } == -1 {

        return None;

    }



    let rx_bytes = if_data.ifi_ibytes as f32;

    let tx_bytes = if_data.ifi_obytes as f32;

    let total_bytes = rx_bytes + tx_bytes;



Some(total_bytes / interface.addr.netmask())
```

```
}
```

In the above, the get_network_utilization function takes the name of the network interface to monitor as a parameter. It retrieves a list of network interfaces and their IP addresses using get_if_addrs. It then filters the list to find the specified interface. Using the libc::if_name2index function, it retrieves the interface index and uses libc::sysctlbyname to get network statistics for the specified interface. The function calculates the total bytes transmitted and received by the interface and divides it by the interface's netmask to get the network utilization percentage.

We can use the notify-rust library to send desktop notifications when network utilization exceeds a specified threshold. To use notify-rust, add it to your Cargo.toml file:

```
[dependencies]

notify-rust = "4.0"
```

We can then use the following code to send a notification when network utilization exceeds the specified threshold:

```rust
use notify_rust::Notification;


fn send_notification() {

    Notification::new()

        .summary("High network utilization")

        .body("The network utilization has exceeded the specified threshold")

        .show()

        .unwrap();

}
```

In this implementation, the send_notification function creates a new desktop notification using notify-rust. It sets the notification summary and body using the summary and body methods and displays the notification using the show method.

To summarize, we set the name of the network interface to monitor and the utilization threshold. We then enter an infinite loop that periodically retrieves the network utilization percentage using the get_network_utilization function. If the utilization exceeds the specified threshold, a desktop notification is sent using the send_notification function. The loop then pauses for 10 seconds before repeating.

Monitoring Latency, Packet Loss and Jitter

Monitoring quality indicators for a network involves tracking metrics such as latency, packet loss, and jitter. In the below sample, we will describe how to monitor these indicators using Rust and the pingr crate.

'pingr' crate

The pingr crate is a Rust library that provides functionality for sending ICMP ping requests and measuring the round-trip time (RTT). To use this library, add it to your Cargo.toml file:

```
[dependencies]

pingr = "0.2.0"
```

Sending Ping Requests

To measure latency, we can send ICMP ping requests to a remote server and measure the time it takes for the server to respond. The pingr library provides a Ping struct that we can use to send ping requests and measure the RTT.

Below is a quick program that sends a single ping request to a remote server:

```
use pingr::Ping;



fn main() {

    let address = "google.com";

    let timeout = std::time::Duration::from_secs(5);
```

```rust
    match Ping::new(address, timeout) {

        Ok(mut ping) => {

            match ping.send() {

                Ok(result) => println!("RTT: {:.2} ms",
result.rtt.as_millis() as f32),

                Err(e) => println!("Error sending ping
request: {}", e),

            }

        },

        Err(e) => println!("Error creating ping object:
{}", e),

    }

}
```

In the above, we set the address of the remote server we want to ping and the timeout duration. We then create a new Ping object using the Ping::new method and send a single ping request using the Ping::send method. If the ping request is successful, we print the RTT in milliseconds. If the ping request fails, we print an error message.

Continuously Monitoring Latency

To continuously monitor latency, we can wrap the ping functionality in an infinite loop and periodically send ping requests.

Below is a similar program that can monitor latency:

```rust
use pingr::Ping;

use std::{thread, time};
```

```rust
fn main() {

    let address = "google.com";

    let timeout = std::time::Duration::from_secs(5);

    let threshold = 100.0;


    loop {

        match Ping::new(address, timeout) {

            Ok(mut ping) => {

                match ping.send() {

                    Ok(result) => {

                        let rtt = result.rtt.as_millis()
as f32;

                        println!("RTT: {:.2} ms", rtt);


                        if rtt > threshold {

                            send_notification();

                        }

                    },

                    Err(e) => println!("Error sending
ping request: {}", e),

                }

            },
```

```rust
            Err(e) => println!("Error creating ping
object: {}", e),

        }


        thread::sleep(time::Duration::from_secs(10));

    }

}


fn send_notification() {

    println!("High latency detected");

    // send notification code here

}
```

After running this program, we set the address of the remote server we want to ping, the timeout duration, and the latency threshold. We then enter an infinite loop that sends periodic ping requests using the Ping::send method. If the RTT of a ping request exceeds the latency threshold, we call the send_notification function to send an alert. We then pause for 10 seconds using the thread::sleep method before repeating the loop.

Monitoring Packet Loss and Jitter

To monitor packet loss and jitter, we need to extend our ping functionality. Packet loss can be calculated by counting the number of unsuccessful ping requests over a period of time, while jitter can be calculated by measuring the variability in RTTs.

Following is a quick program to monitor latency, packet loss, and jitter:

```rust
use pingr::Ping;

use std::{thread, time};
```

```rust
fn main() {
    let address = "google.com";

    let timeout = std::time::Duration::from_secs(5);

    let threshold = 100.0;

    let ping_count = 10;

    let mut rtts = vec![];

    let mut lost_packets = 0;


    for _ in 0..ping_count {
        match Ping::new(address, timeout) {
            Ok(mut ping) => {
                match ping.send() {
                    Ok(result) => {
                        let rtt = result.rtt.as_millis() as f32;

                        rtts.push(rtt);

                        println!("RTT: {:.2} ms", rtt);


                        if rtt > threshold {
                            send_notification("High latency detected");
                        }
```

```rust
                },
                Err(_) => {
                    println!("Packet lost");
                    lost_packets += 1;
                },
            }
        },
        Err(e) => println!("Error creating ping
object: {}", e),
    }


    thread::sleep(time::Duration::from_secs(1));
}


let packet_loss_rate = (lost_packets as f32 /
ping_count as f32) * 100.0;

let jitter = calculate_jitter(&rtts);


println!("Packet Loss Rate: {:.2}%",
packet_loss_rate);

println!("Jitter: {:.2} ms", jitter);
```

```rust
    if packet_loss_rate > 5.0 {

        send_notification("High packet loss detected");

    }

    if jitter > 30.0 {

        send_notification("High jitter detected");

    }

}


fn send_notification(message: &str) {

    println!("{}", message);

    // send notification code here

}


fn calculate_jitter(rtts: &[f32]) -> f32 {

    if rtts.len() < 2 {

        return 0.0;

    }


    let mut diffs = vec![];

    for i in 1..rtts.len() {

        diffs.push((rtts[i] - rtts[i - 1]).abs());
```

```
    }


    diffs.iter().sum::<f32>() / diffs.len() as f32

}
```

In the above, we send multiple ping requests in a loop and store the RTTs in a vector. We count the number of lost packets and calculate the packet loss rate as the percentage of lost packets. We calculate jitter as the average absolute difference between consecutive RTTs. If the packet loss rate or jitter exceeds specified thresholds, we send notifications using the send_notification function.

Summary

In this chapter, we learned the concept of network performance monitoring, which involves tracking various indicators to ensure that a network is performing optimally. We explored three main types of indicators: availability, utilization, and quality.

For availability monitoring, we looked at how to use Rust and its libraries to track metrics such as uptime and downtime. We explored the tokio library and how it can be used to implement asynchronous network monitoring. For utilization monitoring, we learned how to use Rust and its libraries to track metrics such as network bandwidth and CPU usage. We explored the psutil and systemstat crates, which can be used to retrieve system statistics. And, for quality monitoring, we looked at how to use Rust and its libraries to track metrics such as network latency.

We explored the pingr crate, which provides functionality for sending ICMP ping requests and measuring the round-trip time (RTT). We also discussed the benefits of network performance monitoring for networking professionals. Monitoring network performance helps identify and resolve issues in the network, improves network efficiency, and increases overall network reliability.

And, this is where we wrap this book to let you practice all the learnings of this book into the real world. All the best!

Index

271

P

Q

S

T

U

V

W

Epilogue

As we conclude our book "Rust for Network Programming and Automation," I'd like to express my heartfelt gratitude for joining me on this educational adventure. I'm Gilbert Stew, and it's been a pleasure to guide you through the complexities of network programming with Rust 1.68. This second edition aimed to bridge gaps, meet expectations, and provide a comprehensive, up-to-date resource to help you maximize Rust's potential for network programming and automation.

Based on the information we've covered, it's clear that network programming is both a challenging and rewarding field. From the fundamentals of TCP/IP to advanced packet manipulation and analysis techniques, we have delved deeply into the core concepts that power modern networks. Understanding these fundamentals is critical, and I hope that the clear explanations and practical examples provided in this book have solidified your understanding.

One of the most significant improvements in this edition was our emphasis on network automation. Automating network tasks is critical in today's fast-paced, cloud-based world. We researched how to automate various network configurations and tasks using Rust's powerful libraries such as rusoto and pnet, ranging from IP address management to AWS virtual private cloud configuration.

The importance of security has been emphasized multiple times in this book. We talked about secure socket programming, detecting network threats using packet analysis, and monitoring network performance to identify and resolve potential problems. Monitoring network performance is another critical aspect we've looked into in depth. We have learnt to track KPIs like jitter, packet loss, and latency with the help of libraries for collecting and analyzing network traffic and tools like notify-rust.

The practical examples and hands-on approach were created to teach you real-world skills that you can immediately apply to your projects. Whether you're developing network applications, troubleshooting network issues, or automating network tasks, the knowledge in this book will help you succeed. Throughout this book, I attempted to provide a balanced mix of theory and practice, ensuring that you understand not only how to perform various network programming tasks, but also why they are important. Rust's safety, performance, and concurrency features make it an excellent choice for network programming, and I hope this book has adequately demonstrated its capabilities.

In creating this second edition, I attended to your feedback and worked hard to improve and expand the content. Addressing gaps and meeting your expectations were top priorities, and I believe this edition provides a more complete learning experience. Thank you for selecting "Rust for Network Programming and Automation" as your guide. I wish you the best of luck in your future endeavors and look forward to seeing the amazing network solutions you'll build with Rust.

Thank You

Made in United States
Orlando, FL
04 December 2024